Theodora:

*How I Survived a WW2 Japanese Prison Camp,
Fled Indonesian Extremists,
and Escaped the Great Dutch Flood*

By Theodora Kleisma

With Lorilee Craker

Chapbook Press

Schuler Books
2660 28th Street SE
Grand Rapids, MI 49512
(616) 942-7330
www.schulerbooks.com

ISBN 13: 9781943359806

Library of Congress Control Number: 2017957747

Copyright © 2017 Theodora Kleisma
All rights reserved.

No part of this book may be reproduced in any form without express permission of the copyright holder.

Printed in the United States by Chapbook Press.

DEDICATION

This book is dedicated to my children; Errol, Jeffrey, Shirley, Roy, Glenn, Dorris and Irene. Also to my grandchildren and great-grandchildren and to any future generations to come of my family.

ACKNOWLEDGEMENTS

The idea for writing my life's story was a dream of mine for well over 50 years. But not until my youngest son, Glenn, gave me the inspiration and encouragement did this project get started and now is completed.

My life's journey has had so many ups and downs, twists and turns that I am constantly amazed at how God's love and protection has allowed me to survive the life-threatening, disaster-destroying, relationship-breaking events of my life. He has guided me to a safe haven in which I live now; enfolded by the love of my children and their families. What an amazing blessing this is for me!

It is and always has been God's love that has sustained me, given me hope for the future, and a dream to be a better person than who I was yesterday.

My prayer is that this memoir of my life will somehow encourage others to persevere and hold on to God's unchanging hand. He is faithful to see you through whatever you may have experienced or be facing at this point in your life.

Remember His promise in Romans 8:28: "And we know that in all things God works for the good of those who love Him, who have been called according to His purpose."

A special thanks goes to Lorilee Craker for helping me write this book (I talked and shared my story and she wrote), and to my daughter Shirley who was there every step of the way to help me express myself when I couldn't find the exact or correct English words to describe a situation or event. Thank you both so much for allowing this dream of mine to become a reality.

Chapter 1

Three times in my life, I lost everything.

Well, really four times if you count the worst loss of all—the loss of my family.

Here I am, though, still standing after almost a century of survival. "I'm still here," I often tell people, and no one is more surprised than me.

My story is not just one of loss, however. It's about gaining, too, increasing my faith and enlarging my soul. They say suffering enlarges your soul, if you do it right. If you submit to God and allow Him to help you forgive, that is.

Forgiveness changed everything for me, and I hope my story stirs forgiveness in your heart, too. I hope it increases your faith in the God who has been with me through all my trials and joys.

I hope you will see more clearly how God is at work in your life, from the very beginning before you were even born.

The beginning of *my* story dates back more than 350 years to the Spice Islands of the Indonesian archipelago and the wars that ensued over their control. No one who knows me is surprised that my origins are rooted in the Spice Wars! My life has had plenty of spice and too much war.

Now called the Maluku Islands or the Moluccas in Indonesia, these lush, green islands were known as the Spice Islands due to the nutmeg, mace and cloves that were once exclusively found there. The presence of these spices kindled colonial interest from Europe in the 16th century. (One of those islands is the island of Ambon, and part of my later story's thread is woven there.)

The first exchange between Europeans and the peoples of Indonesia began in 1512 when Portuguese traders, led by Francisco Serrão, wanted to gain control of the nutmeg, cloves, and cubeb pepper in Maluku. Spice traders from the Netherlands, the other country in which I have roots, followed in 1596.

That first Dutch expedition lost half its crew, murdered a Javanese prince and lost a ship, but returned to the Dutch Republic with a load of spices. They made so much money off that boatload of spices that all they could do was send more boats. (I am very good with money; I get it from the Dutch!)

In 1602, the Dutch established the Dutch East India Company. It was much more than a company though. The Netherlands could see that huge profits awaited whoever gained control of this area. So the Company was given almost as much power as a government, including the ability to wage war, imprison and execute convicts, negotiate treaties, coin money, and establish colonies. Indeed, even after the Company went bankrupt and dissolved in 1800, the government of the Netherlands established the Dutch East Indies as a nationalized colony.

The Dutch ruled from 1600 until 1949, and even during the early years there were many marriages between indigenous people and the Dutch. This despite the fact that Company leaders tried to keep the colony purely Dutch. Orphan girls and single women from the Netherlands were sent to Batavia (now Jakarta) by the boatload. The single women were brought over to raise the orphan girls to become East India brides! Those poor girls had no choice, and neither did some of the native girls and women who were compelled to marry Dutch traders, sailors, accountants and adventurers.

History teaches us that any time there is a European colonial power, a new ethnic group is inevitably born. I was to descend from the new ethnic group born of native Indonesians and Dutch colonist settlers.

The children of the mixed-race marriages are my ancestors. I am an Indo.

What's an Indo, you ask?

"Indo is a term used to describe Eurasian people who were a migrant population that associated themselves with and experienced the colonial culture of the former Dutch East Indies, a Dutch colony in Southeast Asia that became

Indonesia after World War II." (Indo People—Wikipedia)

My two grandfathers were both born in the Netherlands and came to the East Indies as part of the Dutch military. My grandmother and namesake, Theodora, was born in the East Indies, but she was half Belgian. The Belgian part comes in through the other Europeans who made up the Dutch East India Company. Given the small population of their country, the Dutch had to fill out their recruitment for Asia by looking for immigration candidates in other regions of north-western Europe.

In addition to the Dutch, there were Germans, French, Scots, English, Danes, Flemings, and Walloons that made up half of the Dutch East Indies Trading Company. Europeans living in Batavia also included Norwegians, Italians, Maltese, Poles, Irish, Spaniards, Portuguese, and Swedes. (The number of Swedes traveling to the East on Dutch ships numbered in the thousands. My nephew, who was once an ambassador from the Netherlands to the United States, always maintained that we had some Swedish blood. In winter 2017, I took a DNA test from National Geographic that confirmed I had a little bit of Scandinavian blood.)

And thus, an Indo-European society developed in the East Indies. Although most of its members became Dutch citizens, our culture was Eurasian in nature, with focus on both Asian and European heritage.

By the time I was born in 1926, there were more than 240,000 people with European legal status in the colony, still making up less than half of one percent of the population. Almost 75 percent of these Europeans were Indos, like me and my family.

I was to learn throughout my life that being Indo had its own specific blessings and its own particular burdens. I look Asian but I have always felt Dutch. I'm sure most Indos have felt the same way as I did.

Many white Dutch people considered us less important than themselves, as we originated from the indigenous, 'second class' world. Later, when Japan invaded our country in World War II, the Japanese also considered us inferior Asians. So you see, we were always an in-between group, with one foot in Europe and one foot in Asia. This is part of the Indo's identity—the questions of who we are and where we belong **always a** part of us.

As a mixed-race girl coming of age in wartime, my clashing bloodlines would be the cause of much challenge, danger and loss in my life. I would see far more tragedy, violence, and injustice than anyone should ever see. I would lose someone who meant everything to me—my father. This loss would stay with me for the rest of my life.

But God was working in my life, bringing good out of bad and planting seeds of hope in my darkest hours.

Chapter 2

I was born on March 27, 1926, **in Meulaboh in Aceh** on the island of Sumatra, famous for its coffee and tigers. Known in ancient times as the "Island of Gold" for its gold deposits, my birthplace has always been an exotic place of adventure and wildness.

The largest island in **the Indonesia Archipelago** (and the 6th biggest in the world), few islands in the world tempt adventurers quite like the wild land of Sumatra. A landmass of astonishing beauty, it brims with life under the power of nature. Volcanic eruptions, earthquakes and tsunamis are commonplace. Volcanoes huff and puff while standing watch over the bluest lakes. Orangutan-filled jungles accommodate tigers, rhinos and elephants. And down at sea level, perfect, deserted beaches wait to be explored and enjoyed. What a place to be born!

My parents were wonderful people. My father was named Emile Julius Johanzoon. He was born in 1896, and his parents died in an earthquake when he was two years old. He grew up on the island of Ambon with his aunt and uncle who adopted him. They became my Oma and Opa.

My mother was named Maria Francisca Oostvogels. She was only sixteen when she and my dad married, something that sounds strange to us now but was very common in that place and day.

I am named partly after her mother, my Oma Theodora, who was part Belgian and part Indonesian. As a girl, my Oma and her brother ran away from their mean stepmother to a Catholic convent, where my grandfather met and married her.

My mom was Catholic and my dad was Protestant. They raised me and my siblings to believe in a loving God who cared for His children.

I had an older brother, Gustaaf, whom I never met. He was born to my parents four years before I was born, and died at ten months of age from pneumonia. My dad always believed in the power of prayer, so he prayed and prayed for another child because it seemed as if my mother could not get pregnant again after Gustaaf died.

"If you answer my prayer and give us a child, I will honor you in his or her name," my father prayed. He had a name all picked out: Theodore for a boy and Theodora for a girl, because both names mean "gift of God." The Almighty answered my father's prayers and I was born, Theodora Francisca Johanzoon. My father kept his promise to God in the naming of his child.

My father, Emile, had risen in the ranks as an officer in the KNIL (Royal Netherlands Indonesian

Military) and was already a sergeant. When I was just a baby, he was transferred and we moved to Malang on the island of Java.

Malang is the second largest city in East Java, which today has a rapidly growing population of about 1.2 million.

Though not as exotic a locale as the island of Sumatra, Malang is a city of great historical significance. It dates back from the 8th century when it was the seat of government for the ancient Kanjuruhan and Singhasari kingdoms. It is a city full of ancient Hindu relics and beautiful Dutch colonial architecture, with bright pink bougainvillea climbing everywhere. The city was popular with the Dutch colonists due to its cool climate, gorgeous mountain setting and easy access to the main trading port city of Surabaya, where part of my future story would take place.

Modern Malang, although very urban, has retained much of its historical character. Although I have not been there in many years, I read that my hometown remains colorful and vital, and is regarded as by far the most attractive city in the East Java region. Later, one of my children would be born there.

Malang Regency (or subdivision of a province) is located between two groups of mountains with Mount Semeru, the highest mountain on Java, and

Bromo-Tengger-Semeru National Park to the east. For a time, we lived in the mountains and I remember their stunning beauty.

The beaches were close by, and we loved to go there as a family almost every weekend and play in the sand by turquoise waves. Our favorite beach was in Wendet, although I can't remember quite how to spell it. There were thousands of monkeys there as there are on every beach in the Indies. They would swing in trees and shriek, wild and free, and play under the waterfalls.

As a little girl I would stare as the two biggest monkeys sat on each side of the waterfall, watching everything like a king and queen. The monkeys would steal the bananas right out of your bag if you were not careful.

We would also sometimes see Indonesian water buffalo. Locals would herd hundreds of buffalo along the country roads. They would keep them in long straight lines, taking them to pasture on the edges of the city. Sometimes children would hop on their backs and ride them, balancing on their protruding ribs to avoid the big yellow ticks on their bodies. Really, my childhood was like an open-air zoo, with the animals free to roam around and entertain us. We were wild and free as children, too.

Before the war, when I was a young teenager, I would ride my bicycle to the beach, a journey of about an hour. On the way there was a Hindu Temple in Lawang, where one could make wishes at the fountain. I remember wishing that I would pass my exams to advance into high school, and I did!

At the beach, there would be boys and girls, ukuleles and music under the stars as the waves rolled in. For many people, the beaches of Indonesia are a "bucket list" vacation of a lifetime, but for me it was simply my home. Before the war, we loved our beautiful island: a tropical dream of white sand beaches, craggy mountains and plush green forests.

Before the war, everything was beautiful.

That's how I look back at my life—before and after the war.

Before the war my family led a very comfortable, even pampered, life. **There was me, my younger sister Toet, (Theresia Geertruida, born a year and a half after me, on September 15,1927), and our Chinese younger brother, Ed, born February 2, 1933 who was adopted by our parents at five days old. In** those days, most parents didn't tell their children that they were adopted. Both his parents had disappeared, though I don't know why. When he was still a baby, his biological grandfather found out who we were and came to our house, wanting to make sure that his grandson had been adopted by a good family.

Ed's adoption was a big secret. But when we were older I felt that he should know and I told him. Of course, he was very shaken by this news (although I wonder if he knew on some level; he looked very Chinese and therefore quite different from our decidedly mixed Eurasian looks). When I told him the secret, he locked himself in the shed for a week, only coming out to sneak something from the kitchen to eat. He finally came out for good one day and said, "I am a part of this family, and that's that." I always loved him like my own flesh and blood brother and still do. He lives in the Netherlands and I still speak to him as often as I can.

Our family lived in a large stucco house in a Dutch neighborhood in Malang, near the eastern end of the island of Java in what is now Indonesia. Our house was large, and we had many servants. This was typical for many European families on the island. We had a cook (*Kokkie*), a maid (*Baboe*, although the term means "slave" and is now considered to be a slur); a butler (*Djongos*), a gardener, and more servants. I never thought about what it meant for them that Europeans had taken over their country.

As I have said, I was raised mostly as a Dutch girl even though I looked Asian. We spoke Dutch and thought of the Netherlands as "back home," even though none of us had been born there except my two grandfathers.

We didn't question our mixed race at all. We also didn't socialize with Indonesians, even though we were all part Indonesian. Really, the Indos were kind of snooty in those days. We were brainwashed, I guess. We thought on some level we were better than the native Indonesians. In my mind, I was a totally free person, yet native Indonesians had been colonized and oppressed for hundreds of years. I see now that this included my Indonesian ancestors. One part of my racial identity had oppressed the other.

Today I recognize that both cultures were and are an inseparable part of me. Much later, when I lived in the United States, my husband would ask me, "Well what are you thinking today? Dutch or Indonesian?" He meant was I thinking like a Dutch woman or an Indonesian woman. It was a fair question, and my "thinking" changed from day to day.

Still, it took many years for me to understand my dual identity. Even as a grown woman after the war, my identity was strongly Dutch. When I was first married, natives who lived in caves would come to our house and ask for food. I remember they would bring us pieces of rock that they promised would bring good luck. My first husband, also an Indo, spoke very good Indonesian but he was very black and white about some things. He felt superior to the natives, and didn't give them any food. He always sent them away sternly. I would come to realize that the people we were sending away were really our people, too.

But those thoughts were far from my mind as a child living a wonderful, secure life with two parents who loved me. My mother was a good mother and a good cook. She was a gutsy lady, a trait she passed on to me and one I would dearly need in the troubles to come.

My mother made the most wonderful *Soto Ajam* soup, a beloved Indo recipe. I still make it today and it is one of my favorite recipes to cook for my family. (See the recipe at the back of the book.)

And oh—the fruit! Have I mentioned how lovely the fruit was? The fruit was always abundant and fresh, and we had all we could eat of the sweetest mangoes and the biggest, reddest papayas. I still eat mangoes and papayas sometimes, but they are not nearly as fresh as the ones we could pick off a tree or buy at the market anytime we wanted to. My friend Ernie is Indonesian and she goes back once a year and makes me so jealous talking about all the fresh fruit!

If you ever get the chance to bite into a red, juicy, fresh Indonesian papaya plucked right off the tree, please think of me but don't tell me. I would be too jealous!

Yes, before the war there was an abundance of every kind of food, not just fruit.

We would get regular visits from peddlers who were either Chinese or Indonesian. They would push their carts laden with goodies for sale. Fried dumplings, egg rolls! It was all so delicious and makes my mouth water just to remember. My mother was especially tempted by the peddlers' offerings. My father would tease her all the time that she was busting the household budget with her treat purchases!

We had a friend who was an Arabian man and who sold horses. He had a harem of maybe ten wives. My family was often invited over there for dinner and we eagerly accepted, knowing what a feast was in store for us. The men ate first, then the children and the wives ate last! Our Arabian friend would pop up later in my family's story.

For a while we lived in Toeren, in the mountains, while my Dad was an itinerant evangelist. I would join him as he traveled to various remote villages, preaching the Gospel to all who would hear.

He would tell the people, "If you don't know how to pray, you just need to know one word: 'Help!' Pray 'Lord, help me.'"

I still pray that prayer to this day. Even now, when I can't find something I have misplaced, I ask God to help me!

My father loved living in the country. There were mangoes and papayas hanging off every tree. There was durian, too, which you may not have heard of but is referred to in Southeast Asia as the "king of fruits." It's also the stinkiest of fruits, too, if you've ever smelled a whiff of it.

My mother actually hated living in the country. She loved people and socializing and neither one was in ample supply in the mountains. But for the most part, we Johanzoons were very happy together, the five of us, before the war came and changed everything.

Chapter 3

The war had been going on in Europe since September 1939 when Adolf Hitler, leader of Germany, trooped his army into Poland. The following May, the Netherlands, our home country, fell to him. It was unfathomable that the Netherlands should fall to such a monster, and we were very shaken by this.

Things were heating up closer to home as Japan, fueled by victories in China and on the mainland of Southeast Asia, started focusing on the East Indies, our home. It was decided that my mother, **Toet, Ed and I** would be sent to live with our aunt and uncle in Semarang. My uncle, who was more Indonesian than Dutch, worked as a controller, or accountant, for the Japanese. My parents hoped that they would be more lenient with him and his family, including us. For a whole year, we were hidden from view, essentially trapped within the confines of my aunt and uncle's home and walled gardens. I was between fourteen and fifteen, and Toet thirteen-and-a-half. We lived that way for about a year.

During the year we were in exile, tensions had risen dramatically. The United States countered Japanese aggression by cutting off shipments of scrap iron, steel and oil, resources Japan needed to drive its war and enlarge its empire in the Pacific. The stopping of shipments made Japan more determined than ever to get its hands on the lucrative oil reserves in the East Indies.

Right before the Japanese invasion, we listened to the news on the radio and we got increasingly scared that the Japanese were going to attack us. One thing I remember hearing on the radio is that Princess Juliana of the Netherlands was taken to Canada with her daughter, Beatrix, during the war for their safety. For some reason, this gave me a little bit of comfort. At least the princess and her little girl were safe. **(Queen Wilhelmina went to England and stayed there for the duration of the war, broadcasting on radio** *Oranje* **to bolster the morale of her fellow Dutchmen. Her daughter and family went to Canada.)**

As the conflict rose in the fall of 1941, our government began preparing people in the East Indies for possible war.

All over the region there were huge towers with sirens on them. Whenever that siren went off, it was a signal for everyone to take cover. These practice drills could happen at any time—when we were eating breakfast, sitting in the garden, or sleeping in our beds. The first time we heard the sirens, I was in my aunt and uncle's home with them, my mother, sister and brother. Father was in a secret location with the KNIL. We had no idea where he was or what was happening to him.

We all ran and hid under our beds, shaking with fear. Of course, our beds would have done nothing if a bomb had hit us. Indeed, we are lucky no bombs ever did hit us. When the sirens went off, our terror escalated. How soon before the Japanese would attack our home?

Things started to worsen when Japan surprised the Americans by bombing their naval base at Pearl Harbor, Hawaii, in December 1941. This was quickly followed by attacks on Hong Kong, the Philippines, and other bases in the Western Pacific. It was only a matter of time before they came after us, too.

After Japan attacked Pearl Harbor, the Netherlands Indies was the first of the Allies to declare war on Japan. The German occupation of the Netherlands put an end to the Dutch foreign policy of neutrality. The upshot was that the Netherlands Indies became part of the alliance against imperialistic Japan.

In January 1942, Japanese troops occupied the island of Tarakan in the most important oil development area of the East Indies. Barely two months later, on March 7, 1942, the Royal Netherlands Indies Army, the KNIL, surrendered. The forces, including my father, could not fight back adequately against the well-equipped modern army of the emperor Hirohito. The Dutch had badly underestimated Japanese power, and were convinced that the British, American and Australian forces would be greater than the Japanese army. They could not have been more wrong. My father was captured along with thousands of other KNIL.

Really, the Dutch and the other Western allies were humbled by the strong and organized Japanese war machine. This upset gave the Indonesian nationalist movement its chance to overthrow their colonial Dutch masters. But they too would discover Japanese rule was harsh. Many Indonesians would suffer terribly through forced labor and starvation. What they did not realize at the time was that the Japanese considered other Asian peoples inferior and only useful to make the empire bigger.

On March 9, 1942, the Japanese took control of Java. I would turn sixteen in eighteen days.

Our first sighting of the Japanese were soldiers in trucks riding around our neighborhood like they owned the place. They looked different from us, not just in their facial features but in their unmistakable uniforms of dark navy blue. They wore big caps with gold braid trim, and their boots came up to their knees. Everything about them frightened me. To me, they looked mean and menacing. I shivered whenever I looked at them.

While the war rolled on towards us, things had begun to shift as far as who held the power over the Dutch East Indies. Was it the Dutch or the native Indonesians? This swing in power was to be significant in our lives.

We didn't know it at the time, but the Japanese invaders had persuaded the native population to cooperate with them by allowing their leader, a Javanese man named Sukarno, to create a new government free of the Dutch but accountable to the Japanese. To keep the Dutch from getting in the way of their new control, the Japanese created internment camps. There were to be several hundred of these prison camps across the East Indies.

The Japanese government in Tokyo really wanted all Indo Europeans sent to concentration camps, but the local occupiers so far had not been able to enforce that. They didn't like the Indos any more than they did the full-blooded Dutch. It had been decided that the Indo Europeans would be divided into so-called "blood categories" depending on the percentage of Indonesian blood in their veins.

Indo Europeans with more than 50% Dutch blood would be sent to concentration camps, so me and my family qualified under this category. We were sent to a local concentration camp immediately. All told, 300,000 of us Europeans and Eurasians were forced to live in the camps.

When we were forced to go to that first camp, *Sompoklama*, in Semarang, we sent word home to Malang to let all our servants go, and we gave our furniture and animals to our Arabian friend for safekeeping. The plan was that he would keep the furniture until the war was over. When I look back now I wonder how we could have imagined that life would ever be "back to normal" again.

One positive was that Ed was still a little boy, and therefore could come to the camp with me, my mother and **Toet.** Some camps were for women, others were for men. Boys ten years and older were forced to go to camps for men. Can you imagine letting your **ten**-year-old son go off to a concentration camp alone with a bunch of strangers? We were grateful Ed could be with us **since he was only nine.**

The first camp, *Sompoklama,* was not nearly as terrible as what was to come. We lived in the front room of a big house, with a shared kitchen in the back. We had been able to bring some clothing and bedding so we were not terribly uncomfortable; displaced, yes, but not starving or diseased. At least not yet. We even had school where we learned German and French, and had enough to eat on a daily basis.

Most of the women, including my mother, had always had servants to do the cleaning, cooking and laundry. But they knew if they wanted food to eat, clean clothes to wear and a neat place to live they would have to do the work themselves. We quickly learned this too.

Soon after we arrived in the first camp, we saw our father for the last time. As a sergeant in the KNIL military, my dad was one of the first to be taken and later sent to a prison labor camp. We learned that the Japanese High Command on Java had tried to force the KNIL to enlist in the Japanese army. Those who refused were executed, or, like my father, ended up in camps. The Japanese also tried to force the Indos to renounce their allegiance to the Dutch queen and to become Indonesian citizens. Those who refused were also thrown into camps.

My father was among the members of the KNIL to be rounded up and put on a ship, packed like sardines, to the island of Ambon where they were supposed to build an airport for the Japanese.

But before they left, the prisoners of war were marched right out in front of *Sompoklama*. I spotted him first.

"Pappi, Pappi!" I cried out. A Japanese soldier took pity on him and allowed my father to break from the troops to come over to us quickly and say goodbye. He kissed my mother and told her, "Take good care of my two diamonds," meaning my sister and I. Did he know then he would never see us again? He was about to suffer terrible cruelty and deprivations.

First of all, the sanitation at these camps was dreadful. Conditions were filthy by design—our Japanese captors did not want us to survive the experience. Many people contracted dysentery, also known as the "bloody flux," a highly contagious and painful disease that spreads like wildfire in sailing vessels, army camps, and other places where large groups of human beings live together in close quarters with poor sanitation. (As late as the eighteenth and nineteenth centuries, sailors and soldiers were more likely to die from dysentery than from injuries received in battle.)

In these conditions, dysentery was acute. The sickness was usually accompanied by diarrhea (often bloody), swollen legs, high fever and extreme cramping. I remember hearing people scream in pain when we later were interned at *Halmaheira*, our second and final camp.

My father was one of the first to contract dysentery and die at the labor camp in Ambon, known as one of the bloodiest and cruelest of all the camps.

We didn't know it until a few months later, when my mother received a letter saying my father had died. She didn't say anything, she just began weeping. I grabbed the letter and saw the horrible news in black and white. My heart felt as if it was ripped out of my body. I was sixteen, and I had lost the most important man in all the world to me. We all cried our eyes out for some time to come after that.

We didn't expect him to die, not having any clue what a prison camp is really like or the grave dangers it posed to each one of us. The worst part of losing him was after the war, when other fathers and husbands came back to their daughters and wives, but mine didn't. It was 1943, and my father was forty-seven years old at the time of his death.

As the oldest child, I felt a sudden responsibility to take care of my mother.

"Don't worry," I told her very earnestly, "I will work for you." But Dad had left her a good pension, and after the war she was well taken care of for the rest of her life.

At the time of this writing, it's been seventy-four years since my father hugged me goodbye. I think of him every day, and frequently look at his picture which sits in a frame by my bed. Although I miss him still, I feel close to him and know that I will join him and my mother sooner rather than later in Heaven. What a joyful reunion we will experience!

God granted me a beautiful gift, though, to help me remember my father. My grandson Theodore is the spitting image of my dad. They share the same build and coloring and features. I was nearly brought to tears at Theodore's wedding to see him standing up in his suit, taking his vows. He looked so much like my dad! Today, seeing my grandson is like having a little piece of my father still with me.

Chapter 4

By early April 1942, there were a variety of enslavement centers in operation throughout the Dutch East Indies, with hundreds of thousands of people being held against their will by the Japanese.

POW camps, like the one in which my father died, held members of the armed forces of Allied nations, including Dutch, British and other commonwealth forces, Australians, Americans, Africans, Canadians, South Africans, Chinese, Arabs and Malays. Later on, the majority of POWs were sent overseas to work on the infamous Burma-Thailand railroad, or to Japan itself to perform labor on docks and in the coal mines. (Unbeknownst to me, my first husband was one of those prisoners who worked on the Burma-Thailand railroad. But our meeting was yet several years down the road.)

Me, my mother and siblings were interned in what was simply called a concentration camp. Here, all females, boys under age twelve and, in some cases, old men were interned. These camps held inmate populations between 100 and 18,000 and were found on nearly every island all over the Indies, primarily Java and Sulawesi.

The most famous camps were those in Bandung, West Java, which took up most of the city and held nearly 18,000 human beings. The other infamous camp was Cideng camp in Jakarta. In this camp a brutal Japanese camp commander, Capt. Kenichi Sonei, terrorized his prisoners during the last years of the war. After the war, he was executed as a war criminal.

All concentration camp inmates had to work extremely hard. Even women up to age 60 had to perform manual labor. I was thankful that my mother's mother, my Oma, was allowed to stay with my aunt and uncle in their home in Semarang. Opa, though, had been captured and taken to a camp in Ambarawa.

Oma, at least, was safe and would not be forced to endure the grueling conditions of the camps.

Inmates were used as garbage and junk collectors, sewer and drain cleaners, kitchen workers, furniture removers, clerical workers, grass cutters, and laborers to perform other chores outside the camp.

But conditions at Sompoklama were humane and tolerable, at least compared to the second camp: Halmaheira.

After a year at the first camp, we were transported to our second camp, also in Semarang, via overcrowded army trucks. Our trip there only took fifteen minutes or so, but in terms of conditions it was as if we had been transported to a new and horrific planet.

Halmaheira was a much bigger camp than the first one, with much bigger problems. It housed almost 4,000 women and young boys divided among several compounds. We lived in bamboo huts instead of cement dormitories. Our hut housed eight people, including my mother, sister, brother and I. It had a thatched roof and torn and tattered screens, which offered little to no protection from flying insects. There was an open doorway with no door. Everybody slept on the ground on straw mats.

Here there was no place to cook anything because all the cooking for our meager meals was done in the camp kitchen. There was no electricity, but that was okay because daylight lasts a long time in the tropics.

Just as in our first camp, we all had to work. This time, though, the work was much harder labor and on significantly less food.

There were thousands of people to feed, and therefore thousands of wood stoves to feed with wood. One of our chores at Halmaheira was cutting down trees. We went in groups to the forests outside of our camp to cut down small trees with machetes. The daily chopping and dragging took their toll on our hands, elbows, arms and back. One of my most hated jobs was carrying the big cooking drums, around the size of a 55-gallon modern cooking drum. Obviously I couldn't carry one of those heavy drums myself. We worked in groups of four, attaching the drum to two large, sturdy sticks under its handle, with each person taking one end of a stick. It felt like we would never get to the camp kitchen hauling those huge drums on our aching shoulders.

The food at Halmaheira was mostly rice and not enough of that. We would have a little bit of mush and a little bit of bread for breakfast. We ate very little protein, perhaps just a few spoons of ground beef per day. We women were always on the lookout for wild animals we could catch and kill for food. We saw dogs, an occasional cat, monkeys, and turtles in our cooking pots.

One day an older lady was crying. Her job was to serve the meals.

"Why are you crying?" people asked her.

"I have to kill my dog," she said, weeping.

She was an older lady who loved her dog like a child. The Japanese soldiers told her she had to kill her pet and then serve it to the others to eat. In the end, the soldiers beat her dog, torturing it and finally killing it. It was one of the worst things I have ever seen. I'll never forget when this devastated old lady scooped up a bit of ragout, made from her dog, and slopped it on my plate.

But honestly, we were so hungry that we were glad even for this horrible sustenance. We felt sorry for the old lady, while at the same time knowing that things had become so desperate that something normal in our old life, such as a pet dog, was now an unimaginable luxury from a bygone time. We had no way of knowing how long we would be incarcerated, or if we would ever leave the gates of Halmaheira alive. Personally, I was just trying to get through each day. That, and I was trying to keep my mother alive in the best way I could. **Toet,** Ed and I all were.

When we first got to Halmaheira, my mother was in tolerably good health. The Japanese soldiers forced us to march around every day, but she was so stubborn she would find a closet and hide in it. But quickly she began to deteriorate with the oppressive heat and scarcity of quality food. At one point, my mother became so malnourished she developed red spots all over her body. She was skin and bones, close to death from lack of vitamins and protein. We were constantly on the hunt for nourishment for her. We would kill cats and little birds to make broth for her to eat.

Ed would climb up in the trees and beat herons on the branches with a stick. Yes, herons, those long-legged birds that are today a protected species in the United States. Most people would consider them inedible, but to the starving, almost anything is edible. And on the island of Java during World War

II, nothing whatsoever was protected: not birds, not animals, not human beings.

Ed would beat them with a stick until they were senseless, at which point they would fall out of the trees. There would be women standing underneath the tree, fighting each other over the fallen birds. They would literally tear the birds apart because they were so hungry. It was a feeding frenzy of famished humans who would eat anything at all.

I heard a story from one of my fellow survivors about the time she ate something horrible. She and some others from her camp heard a stray cat hissing and went to see what was happening. To their surprise, there was a huge python slithering slowly across the ground. A group of mothers went after the snake, beating it to death with cooking spoons. After killing the snake, they hung it up, stripped off its skin, and divided it between the hungry families. It had been disgusting to eat, she said, but when you're hungry you will eat no matter what.

Probably the worst thing I had to eat in the concentration camp was bats. There were bats flying around the camp, in and out of the open doors and windows, and me and my siblings would chase them down with nets and make a soup out of them. We hoped the broth would be sustaining for our mother, who was so frighteningly underfed. We were scared out of our wits just looking at her spindly limbs, hollow cheeks, and red sores all over her body.

It's funny how some foods are considered a delicacy in various cultures, but thought of as inedible in others. You may be served escargot in fancy French restaurants, but in those days we ate "escargot" to avoid starvation. There were snails and slugs all over the place, especially during monsoon season. We would get empty cans from the kitchen and roam around the camp, eyes peeled for the slimy protein sources. They were disgusting to touch, but when boiled and served with our small portions of rice they were quite tasty, believe it or not.

Some survivors of the camps reported eating laundry starch, too. A few enterprising women figured out that if you cooked and cooled the starch, it would thicken like Jell-O. By itself it was tasteless, but mixed with *Sambal*, the little red peppers that grew around the camp, it wasn't too bad and it filled empty bellies for a short time.

I remember that the Japanese gave us buckets of hot red peppers in hopes of killing us. In their minds, we Europeans could not handle the spiciness. But the vitamins in the peppers ended up saving us, or at least saving us from getting Beri-Beri or some of the other diseases that stemmed from vitamin deficiency. So many of my fellow inmates were dying or would die of hunger edema. Their legs and arms were like sticks, their tummies bloated and cheeks puffy. They were in the last stages of Beri-Beri, or starvation. I'll never forget the sight of small children who could barely walk, their frames like small skeletons.

The Japanese would throw all the dead into a mass grave outside the camp—a large hole in the ground dug especially for this purpose. When the war was over, Allied rescue troops would unearth the bodies with all the others and bury them properly in the cemetery outside of town. They would top each of the graves with a nameless white cross. I thank God daily that this was not my fate, or the fate of my mother, sister or brother.

You had to be so resourceful to get enough to eat. Sometimes when I was assigned to "night watch" I would steal cabbages, coconuts and bananas. I would have received a terrible beating if I had been found out, but I was never discovered.

There were no screens on the windows, and nights in the East Indies are buzzing with mosquitos. We were covered in itchy welts, but thankfully none of us ever got malaria, a disease that causes sky-high fevers and violent shakes—even death. We also had terrible bed bugs and lice. They bit you all night long when all you wanted to do was sleep. We were always exhausted, and our bodies were scratched raw.

As far as keeping ourselves clean, that seemed like a distant dream. There were no washers or dryers, or hot water for that matter. Even clean water was hard to come by. Often people would share a laundry tub without changing the water. All our clothes and linens were scrubbed by hand, wrung out, and hung to dry on a clothesline strung around our room.

Some inmates used toilets, which were buckets on raised platforms where everybody could see you do your business. I remember digging my own toilet in the ground, in a bamboo outhouse with a half door. Some of the bigger prisoners had the job of digging out the human waste from these holes and transporting it to dumping stations. This was a constant chore because it didn't take long for the holes and the buckets to be filled, especially since most people were suffering from constant diarrhea. The slop buckets had handles on them, through which a large bamboo pole would be placed. One or more women would take one end of each pole, hanging the pole over their shoulders and lifting the buckets for a long hike in the hot sun to the dumping station ditch at the other end of the camp.

Toilet paper, you ask? Another dream of another lifetime. Our only option was to use rags ripped from our worn-out clothing and wash ourselves with cold water in front of everybody.

There was precious little dignity to be had at Halmaheira.

And the heat—oh, it was just so horribly hot no matter what we were doing, but especially carrying heavy waste buckets, cooking drums, or digging holes. We teenagers would dig holes for the Japanese to hide their machine guns. The size of the holes seemed perfect for a body, which made us think that the Japanese were planning to kill us after the war. Or maybe before the war ended. It could be any day now.

If you didn't listen to and obey the Japanese immediately, they would slap you hard in the face or hit you in the back with the butts of their rifles, sometimes knocking you down. This happened to me a few times but, really, I was one of the lucky ones. Our captors withheld food and medication and treated the prisoners in the most brutal of ways. Many were tortured and raped and beheaded. After all, they had their orders: The Imperial Japanese Army's instructions were to terminate the Western races living on the islands at all costs.

Clothing was always an issue. Usually we only had the clothes we had packed when we left home. Everything was either ripped, threadbare, or too tight. Once in a great while the commandant of Halmaheira allowed the Red Cross to bring clothes to the camp. Visits by the Red Cross were something officially provided for in rules of war called the

Geneva Convention. But the Japanese mostly felt they were above these rules and did not comply. Any "new" piece of clothing was cause for great joy.

It's amazing how everyday life continues even under the most harsh and dangerous of circumstances. There were lots of teenagers at Halmaheira, and we escaped gnawing stomachs and total lack of necessities by being together. We teenagers were still teenagers sometimes. We would laugh and tell jokes as we did our chores.

We took a cue from the native Indonesians and sometimes bathed in the river, using stones to scrub our skin. This was a blessed relief from the filth that caked our bodies. The cool water relieved the scratches and abrasions all over us from clawing at the bug bites.

If only there had been a way to draw spiritual refreshment as well. At the second camp, there was no church and no school. We were forbidden to sing or pray openly. Anyone who risked it was beaten by the soldiers. But they could never stop us from praying inside our hearts. I prayed the prayer my father taught me countless times during my three years in internment camps:

"Jesus, help me!"

Chapter 5

In Halmaheira, the only thing we knew was the life of the camp. We knew zero about what was happening in the outside world, where a world war stormed on, killing millions. When we entered the camps in the spring of 1942, Hitler ruled most of Europe and was fighting the Soviets. Conquest over the Soviets would increase his domain to the borders of Japan's new empire in Asia.

As far as any of us knew, Japan still controlled and overpowered the Pacific region. We didn't know that the war had killed at least fifty million people, mostly non-soldiers, some of whom were interned the way we were in horrible concentration camps. We didn't know about Dachau or Auschwitz or any of Hitler's death camps. We just knew about Halmaheira and Sompoklama and Ambon and Ambarawa.

But the battles raging on far, far away from us would have a great effect on our lives. The war in Europe had finally ended with Germany's surrender on May 7, 1945. Then, in August 1945, the United States dropped two atomic bombs on Japan, killing at least 100,000 people in Hiroshima and Nagasaki. Japan surrendered less than a week later.

There was nothing to prepare us for the Allied planes which suddenly circled overhead, dropping packages into the camp. I was in bed in my hut when I heard the roar of the airplanes, the same kind of roar I used to hear in another lifetime, when Japanese planes were bombing us.

Now instead of scurrying under our beds or into bomb shelters, we women of Halmaheira streamed out into the open. We ran around gathering up the bundles and collecting them into big piles. There was a celebratory mood undampened by the cold-eyed guards, who did not stop us as we tore open the bundles with joy, freely eating the food and even the candy tucked inside. Newly powerless, they were probably in shock. All the guards could do was watch us in silence.

People were weeping and shrieking with shock and excitement. We all ate as much as we wanted to, although most of us got sick afterwards. Our bodies were accustomed to hunger and our digestive systems couldn't handle so much rich food. Some people actually died because their bodies were too weak to deal with the diarrhea and vomiting that eating it caused. It would take time for us to readapt to a normal, healthy intake of food. The Red Cross soon began serving meals and some inmates ate so much they literally dropped dead, their bodies in a state of shock after nearly starving. But thankfully, the majority of us lived on to enjoy these new and longed-for tastes of freedom.

Soon after the first care packages were dropped, the camp commandant assembled the group leaders of the camp and told them that the war was officially over. The Netherlands was once again in control of the Dutch East Indies, even though the Japanese had promised independence for the islands.

As Indos, our celebration was short lived. We had no idea what terrible troubles were around the bend. Have you heard the saying "out of the frying pan, into the fire?" That's what would happen very shortly for all European and mixed-race inhabitants of the East Indies. But for the days following the end of the war, we reveled in our liberation.

Most of the former prisoners remained in camp until our rescuers could figure out a plan for taking care of the sick and getting the rest out of there safely. We didn't know at first that simply walking out of the camp might get us shot—not by the Japanese but by the angry Indonesian extremists.

Within a week or two after the packages were dropped, soldiers parachuted into our camp. They were Gurkhas from Nepal, part of the British forces. They had come to protect us from a new enemy, Indonesian nationalists.

Quickly it became obvious that the Japanese surrender did not mean peace for the Netherlands Indies. The Japanese authorities had promised to grant independence to the Indonesian people, and now that the war was over the Indonesian people were intent on reclaiming their country.

They were intent on independence from us—the Dutch. Nationalist leaders Sukarno and Mohamed Hatta proclaimed this independence on August 17, 1945, two days after liberation day.

We former prisoners in the Japanese internment camps suddenly found ourselves threatened by young revolutionary extremists. Stoked by the Japanese propaganda machine, the native Indonesians had grown increasingly hostile to anyone with any Dutch blood. By the time the war ended, Indos like me were abruptly facing a new war, one just as dangerous—maybe more dangerous.

Halmaheira was surrounded by revolutionaries. They wanted to kill us because we were Dutch, and they wanted to kill the Japanese for breaking their promise of independence. What was supposed to be peacetime quickly turned into a war zone.

Hedwich Freeth, an Indo survivor of the Japanese camps, remembered how bad it got immediately after Sukarno had declared independence for Indonesia:

"When we left the camp, we still saw signs of rebelling Indonesians. Once, on our way to school, we saw people being hung from telephone poles and others getting shot at as they tried to escape through the road ditches. We saw three Indo men hanging from the wires. Their feet, large and bloated, traced circles in the air. Instead of looking at their faces, I watched large black flies crawl out of one man's mouth. We ended up running to school and were asked to lie on the floor because it was so unsafe. At a young age, I began to understand the value of listening, it saved my life many times." (www.theindoproject.org)

Still, despite the terrible new threat of the extremists, my family had much to be thankful for. We had all survived, except for my dear father. Because my aunt and uncle still lived in Semarang, we were able to leave camp and go directly to their house, thankfully unscathed by the extremists outside the camp.

The allies were working hard to reunite prisoners from men's camps with those from the women's camps. One of the hardest things for me was witnessing joyous and tender reunions between other girls and their fathers. My heart was broken to know I would never see my father again on this earth.

But we were to be safely reunited with my Opa, who had been interned in a camp in Ambarawa.

We had seen our Opa once in the last few years. During the war, they transferred the old men to our camp for a week. We had been very sad the last time we had seen him before we were taken, because we had not known if we would see him again. But there he was, calling my grandmother's name. I could hardly believe it.

"Dora! Dora!" I heard him call her. He could barely walk. We walked around camp with Opa, thrilled to see him. He was so proud of us, and we loved our "Oudje," which is an affectionate term for an old man one loved or was very fond of. He had been a bricklayer in the Netherlands and very strong, so it had been difficult to see him in such a weakened state.

In the middle of the night they transferred him, and once again we wondered if we would ever see him again.

Now it was after the war, and it was decided I would accompany my Oma on the long journey from Semarang to Ambarawa to pick up Opa and bring him back to my aunt and uncle's house. I had always been close to my sweet Oma, my namesake. We took a hot bus on the first leg of the journey, filled with sweaty people and even some chickens. But on the way home we decided the bus ride would be too hard on Opa as he couldn't lie down and rest. Me and Oma hired a driver and loaded an emaciated Opa on a cart driven by oxen. It took twelve hours for us to travel through the mountains this way.

My typically jolly, happy Opa was extremely ill with a malnourishment-related disease. He kept soiling himself so Oma would change him and clean him up as best she could, right there in the cart. We finally got to my aunt's house in Semarang, where Opa was cleaned up and laid in a comfortable bed for the first time in three years. We all took very good care of him, but he was too far gone. He was soon dying.

We worried about his eternal destination, for as far as we knew Opa was not a Christian. However, we were comforted by the fact that Opa asked us to pray the "Our Father," the Lord's Prayer, with him over and over. We already knew that he respected the Lord's Prayer. When he had been in our camp briefly, my mother had washed his pants and had fished out a copy of the prayer from his pant pocket.

When he was very close to dying, in the middle of the night, he said he saw two people with no heads. Two of our friends had been beheaded while in a camp.

All of the sudden he spoke the words I will never forget.

"Emile," he said to my father, his son-in-law. They had been very close as father-in-law and son-in-law. "Just wait outside. I'll be there at 11 o clock." He ended up dying very close to 11 a.m. that morning."

These things comforted me and gave me hope that I would see my Opa again one day in Heaven, and that he would be waiting there for me with my father.

Chapter 6

My mother went home to Malang after we were released from Halmaheira and my Opa had died. She found everything eerily empty. Every stick of furniture was gone. Not a single shred remained of our former lives, when we were happily living together as a family in our beautiful home.

And our Arabian friend, the one who had the harem of wives and with whom we had left our things for safekeeping? His house was empty too. We found out later he had been murdered by the Japanese at some point during the war. We believed it was because the Japanese found out he was helping us.

My mother hardly got over the shock of this when she was captured again, this time by the Indonesian extremists. She was once more taken to an internment camp for an indefinite amount of time. It sounds funny to say, but I wasn't terribly upset when we got the news in Semarang that my mother was once more a prisoner. I don't know if I was numb or wild with relief at being out of the Japanese camp, but I took the news quite calmly. She was a very gutsy woman, and I knew she would survive.

With no way to help my mother except to pray for her, I began to carve out a new life for myself in Semarang with my grandmother, aunt and uncle, and sister **and my brother Ed.** I was nineteen years old, and I wanted to make up for lost time and be a teenager.

One day I went with a friend to pick up a paycheck from the train office where he worked. There was an English soldier stationed there who was a corporal in the British army. His name was Jack Henderson, and he looked exactly like Bing Crosby with those bright blue eyes. He was five years older than me.

Sparks flew between us immediately. He asked me out for dinner and dancing, and gave me chocolate on that first date. Very quickly, I found myself falling for him and he for me. We loved to dance to the songs of 1945: "Till the End of Time" by Perry Como; "Saturday Night" by Frank Sinatra; "It's Only a Paper Moon" by Ella Fitzgerald. We danced the night away to them all. But "our song"—"Stardust"—was special. Even to this day when I hear those words—"The melody haunts my reverie, And I am once again with you"—I am back in 1945, in Semarang, in Jack Henderson's arms.

Jack was always so handsome to behold in his British military uniform. My aunt and sister would peek through the blinds of our house and watch me and Jack dance under the moon. Oma would peek too. "So beautiful, those two," she would say in Dutch.

Jack told his mother in England about us via letters. He sent her my picture, and she sent me some silky soft camisoles in a package. Why on earth would Jack's mother send me underwear from England? I have no idea! But it wasn't because she thought I would become her future daughter-in-law. Jack was very kind but had made it clear that he could never marry me because I was not white. I wasn't hurt. I knew the way the English were and, to me, they seemed closed to the idea of marrying someone from another race, at least during that time. Perhaps it was because of this factor that I withheld a part of my heart from him.

When, after a year of dating, he got transferred to India, I was not as crushed as one might imagine I would be. I thought, "at least we had fun."

You must remember that I was kind of wild in those days. We all were, after the war. But then again, I have never forgotten Jack Henderson and still think of him when I hear certain songs. You never forget your first love.

Jack sent me two letters from India. The first one was signed, "Love, Jack." He wondered how I was and said that he missed me. I never replied. You see, I had already met my future husband and had moved on emotionally. We will get to that in a moment.

The second letter from Jack said it all. "I have a feeling you have a new boyfriend..." he wrote. And he signed that second and last letter "wish you luck." I never heard from him again.

After Jack was transferred to India, things became increasingly unstable and dangerous with the extremists. The Allies, with the help of the Red Cross, were attempting to evacuate all Europeans and people of mixed race. Those who had been interned during the war were evacuated first by the Red Cross, which also gave us some money to restart our lives. I remember we were given the choice of Australia, Borneo or Thailand. I chose Thailand. Australia was too far away and Borneo was practically in the East Indies. Thailand was just right. I wanted to get away from Indonesia and my well-meaning but nosy family.

My Oma, aunt and uncle loved me but I was under their thumbs, or at least that's how it felt to an independent girl like me. I wanted to see the world, and here was my chance.

So my best friend Stine, whom I had met after the war in Semarang, and I embarked upon an American ship together bound for Thailand. Stine was an Indo like me. I called her "Spooky" because she looked pale and, well, spooky to me!

We were placed in the lowest class of travel, which did not impress me one bit. After losing everything in the war and nearly starving to death in the camps, I was more than ready to resume the life to which I had become accustomed as a child and teenager. In our third-class "accommodations," everyone had to sleep on the floor and I simply wasn't having it. Stine knew me well. She could sense my restlessness and frustration.

"Uh oh, what are you going to do now?" she asked. Stine understood all too well I *would* do something about it.

I went to the captain and batted my long, black eyelashes at him. "Oh Captain," I said in a sad voice, "I just can't stay in that awful third class. It makes me sick, and I've already been through so much hardship..."

We *were* filthy and there were no showers for the third class. I boldly asked the captain if we could take showers in his stateroom and, amazingly, he agreed!

He allowed us to stay in his quarters because there was plenty of room and he felt sorry for us. He brought Stine and I the delicious food from the first-class dining room. It was a five-day voyage and we stayed in the captain's quarters the whole time, showering regularly and dining on the best food!

I remember the American soldiers teasing me and Stine. They rolled Stine up in a blanket and swung her back and forth, pretending they were going to throw her off the ship. "Don't do it! Stine!" Part of me knew they were just teasing, but another part of me was completely freaked out.

It took five days to get to Thailand. When we got off the ship, that was the end of my luxury accommodations. It was back to sleeping on the floor for me and Stine. All the third-class passengers were taken to a hall where refugees were processed. We were tired, but also keyed up and excited. When it was time to go to bed, sleeping on the floor of the hall with other refugees, we balked. We knew we couldn't sleep, and we *were* in Bangkok after all. They tell me there is a song called "One Night in Bangkok." Have you heard it? The city pulsed with excitement and beckoned two wild teenage girls. We decided to go dancing, all night long.

By this time the captain felt responsible for us. When Stine and I were not accounted for at bedtime, he was very worried that we had been kidnapped. He personally looked for us all night.

When the sun came up after our night of revelry, we went back to the hall, oblivious to the trouble we had caused. As soon as we were spotted, we got called into the captain's office. He was trembling with anger. "That's it," he declared sternly. "No money for you!" (As I said, we were eligible for some humanitarian payments from the Red Cross.)

I climbed into his lap and instinctively played on his sympathies. I sensed that he saw me and Stine as young girls who were wild, yes, but also to be pitied. We were alone, without any parents. We needed a father figure to guide us, and he was doing his best during the short time we were in his sights. That poor captain! We really were two very naughty girls.

"Oh, dear Captain, we are poor. Please give us the money!" I begged him, and I guess it worked. He gave us the money on one condition: That we would be put immediately on a train to a small town where there was a military base. No more dancing the night away in Bangkok for the two of us!

We had no choice but to agree to the captain's ultimatum. And I had no idea that boarding that train would change the course of my life.

Chapter 7

The Thai town where we were sent was called Naka, in Phuket province near Patong Beach. Lots of military people lived there, including someone who was soon to be very important to me.

From the train station, Stine and I jumped in a military truck and were driven to the military base through rugged, jungled terrain. There were bamboo huts everywhere in the lush, green foliage. A handsome soldier was there to greet the truck. When he saw how small I was and how high up off the ground the truck was, he extended his arms to me, grabbed me and lifted me down to the ground.

His name was Lodewijk Schlundt-Bodien, but everyone called him "John."

Stine and I were put up for the night in a bamboo barrack. The next morning there was a knock at our door. It was the handsome soldier who had lifted me down from the truck.

He held a pair of wooden sandals in his hands, which he offered to me. "There are centipedes everywhere," he warned. I thanked him warmly.

"What do I owe you?" I asked.

"Nothing," he said. "But I'd like to take you two girls out for dinner."

And so it began. Stine and I went on a double date with John and his cousin. We walked home together under a huge moon. When he asked me for a second date, I did not hesitate. Was it the moonlight or the way he looked at me with his brown eyes?

It was all very romantic, but I didn't know then that he was still married to his second wife.

With his first wife, Lucy, John had two children: Walter and Bridget. With his second wife, Alma, he had Joanie, who would end up dying of typhoid at the age of nine. I knew none of this.

All I can say is that it was crazy times after the war. We were all looking for a portion of stability and security, and John seemed to offer this to a girl who had been through more instability and trauma in her short life than many people experience in their whole lives. Even when John told me about his wife (right before asking me to marry him), I was unfazed. He told me that his marriage was over before we met, that they were through. I accepted this quite easily. He wrote his wife a letter asking for a divorce, and she agreed. And then John asked me to marry him, a proposal I accepted. It sounds so cut and dried, but it honestly unfolded just like that.

Perhaps I was not thinking clearly after the trauma of the war. He was thirteen years older than me, and maybe I was looking for a father figure. I missed my father dearly, and here was an older man who seemed to want to take care of me.

We remained in Thailand for a couple of months, falling in love and getting more serious.

While getting to know John, I learned that he had been badly injured during his years in a Japanese labor camp in Burma (now Myanmar). A sergeant major in the KNIL, John had been enslaved by the Japanese like my father and many other military personnel. He was one of thousands of prisoners who did hard labor on the notorious Burma-Siam railway, made famous by the 1952 book and 1957 movie "Bridge on the River Kwai" starring William Holden and Alec Guinness.

The bridge was a Japanese undertaking driven by the need for better communications to support the large Japanese army in Burma.

According to the Commonwealth War Graves Commission, during the bridge's construction approximately 13,000 prisoners of war died and were buried along the railway. An estimated 80,000 to 100,000 civilians also died during the project, chiefly forced labor brought from Malaya and our home, the Dutch East Indies. Two labor forces, one based in Siam and the other in Burma, worked from opposite ends of the line toward the center.

Early in his imprisonment, John dug a tunnel under a chain link fence on the grounds of the labor camp but was quickly recaptured and tortured. At one point, he was speared in the leg by a Japanese soldier with a bayonet, an injury which caused him problems for his whole life. In later years if he even watched a movie about the Japanese he would get terrible nightmares.

Unfortunately, the wound on his leg would become infected regularly, a dreadful "souvenir" of his time in the labor camp. Once, while we were dating, the infection became so serious he had to be transferred from our small military outpost to a big hospital in Bangkok.

I followed him to Bangkok so I could be with him as much as possible. We were very serious by that point. Stine came with me to provide moral support, but this time we did not dance the night away. I still don't know how we managed this, but we were put up at the luxurious Trocodero Hotel for a few days while John was being treated. It must have been military connections that got us a room in a place like that.

A travel guide from 1950 (just a few years after our stay there), describes it like this:

"This hotel is situated near the corner of Suriwongse Road and New Road, in the business section of Bangkok, and one of the largest hotels in town. All rooms are fully screened and equipped with ceiling fans. Bath-rooms with running water are attached. Excellent cuisine..."

This writer was right about the "excellent cuisine" part. Exhausted from our twelve-hour journey, I flopped down on the silky bedspread and ordered the unimaginable lavishness of room service. I felt like a queen.

Believe me, window screens, ceiling fans, and attached bathrooms were lovely treats for anyone in those days, especially for two girls living in bamboo barracks in a jungle military outpost. On base, we had to use mosquito netting to avoid malaria, and if nature called in the night we would have to stumble outside to the outhouse.

If you're ever in Bangkok, I hear the Trocodero is still a hotel, though not quite as luxurious as it once was.

Soon after John's hospital stay, the military transferred him back to Indonesia, this time to Surabaya, near where I grew up in Malang.

Surabaya was and is a big, crowded city. Today it's polluted, congested, and has a crazy eight-lane highway that drives visitors to despair. But if you have the patience to look a little deeper, Surabaya has fascinating little corners to explore. Its historic Arab quarter, for example, is an intricate maze leading to a historic mosque. Surabaya also has one of Indonesia's biggest Chinatowns and some impressive Dutch colonial buildings.

I followed my fiancé back to our homeland, despite the dangers that waited for us. Surabaya, which was to be our first home as a married couple and the birthplace of our first two children, was also a hotbed of extremists. In fact, the city is still closely linked to the birth of the Indonesian nation, as it was here that the battle for independence began. The Battle of Surabaya, in the autumn of 1945, was the heaviest single battle of the revolution and became a national symbol of Indonesian resistance. Sukarno himself said, "The city was in pandemonium. There was bloody hand-to-hand fighting on every street corner." To locals, Surabaya is *Kota Pahlawan* (City of Heroes), and statues commemorating independence stand on many street corners throughout.

We were sometimes afraid of the nationalists, but in 1946 we still didn't know how much danger any one of us was in because of our Dutch blood. Perhaps we felt a sense of false security because we lived right next to barracks full of KNIL soldiers. Maybe we were a little bit naïve about what could happen to us there.

John and I got married in 1946, though I can't remember the date. I was twenty years old and he was thirty-three. I needed permission from my mother to get married because in those days you had to be twenty-one to get married without a parent's consent. My mother, who had spent a year in an extremist prison camp but was now released, readily accepted John as a son-in-law despite the fact that he had been married twice already and had several children. Although, later, the two of them would butt heads.

At our wedding, a tiny affair with a justice of the peace officiating, John had two witnesses, one for him and one for me.

We were two people in love that day in Surabaya. As I took my vows, I thought that John would take care of me for the rest of my life, but he would soon disappoint me. Later on, we would disappoint each other.

Chapter 8

One of the hardest things that happened in my early marriage was that John got caught up in smuggling guns. He had child support to pay for his children from his previous marriages, so he was always selling something. He would sell the wild boar he hunted—things like that—and then the nature of his selling became more criminal. He began buying guns and selling them on the black market to the Chinese. The extremists were after the Chinese, so the Chinese wanted weapons but couldn't purchase them. Eventually John was caught and thrown in a military prison. I was extremely upset. We had only been married for about a year and we were still newlyweds. I couldn't believe he would risk so much for money. This man whom I had hoped would care for me had left me alone and pregnant to fend for myself.

Yes, by this point I was pregnant with our first child. At first John refused to admit to the military police that he had been selling guns. I'm not sure why, but his release was contingent on a confession of wrongdoing, even though they had him dead to rights. I finally begged him to confess so he could get out of jail. "Think of the baby," I begged. He confessed and was released just in time for the birth of our child.

One day, when I was about eight months pregnant, John and I had a disagreement. We had plans to go out that night, and I was looking forward to getting out of the house. Then John got a call saying the soldiers in the barracks next door would be coming over for some training instead. Our night out was off.

Miffed, I decided to take a walk in the field across the street. I was walking down the road near our house in the tall grass. I had sandals on. Suddenly a large snake, measuring three or four inches in diameter with red rings around its body, **most likely a Coral Snake,** slid over my foot and bit me on the big toe. The bite itself didn't hurt that badly, but I knew instantly that the baby and I were in big trouble. The poison spread through my body quickly, and a hard lump formed in my groin.

I ran home and burst into John's training with the soldiers. "I was bit by a snake! I have to go to the hospital!" John apparently couldn't leave his training session, but one of the soldiers rushed me to the hospital in a military Jeep. There the doctors said I had two choices: to have a shot that was an antidote for the poison but would cause me to go into immediate, premature labor, or allow the poison to spread and kill both of us. I had no choice at all. I received the shot and the lump in my groin dissolved.

My firstborn son, Errol, arrived the next day, January 19, 1948, born at home. In those days there were no hospital births, just home births. I named him Errol after an Australian movie star, Errol Flynn, who achieved fame in Hollywood for his romantic swashbuckler roles in films. I always liked his nice little mustache. (I would go on to name all my children after movie stars!)

My sweet little Errol had to struggle from his first moments. He was born too soon, and the midwife pulled him out hard by his head because he wasn't coming out properly. If I had given birth today, my pregnancy could probably have been prolonged by modern medical practices, or he could have received the oxygen he needed even if he had been born at eight months, but in January of 1948, there was nothing they could do.

I knew when he didn't cry at birth that he was in grave danger. The midwife sucked something out of his nose and finally he began to cry, but not like a strong baby cried. He was sickly from the start, and didn't want to eat much at all. I was worried, but also naïve. What did a young mother like me know about how a newborn was supposed to behave? Still, my instincts told me that something was wrong with my baby boy.

John didn't seem to share my worries. As soon as it was clear in his mind that the baby and I would be okay, he left for a multi-day hunting trip in search of wild boar. (He loved to hunt and fish more than almost any other activity, and continued this when we immigrated to the United States. While still in Indonesia, he taught me how to skin deer, process wild boar, and kill a fish with my bare hands.)

I was upset with him, but too consumed with my baby to really let him have it. My mother, on the other hand, was infuriated. She screamed and yelled at him, telling him off for leaving me and the baby.

The next day Errol was worse, skinny and listless. I knew enough to know he needed help. I was so scared I would lose him.

My mother and I bundled up baby Errol and brought him to the Salvation Army hospital. I remember we shared a room with a beggar and her baby. Errol was nursing properly but I pumped my milk in the hopes that he would take a bottle.

My nurse was from the island of Ambon, where there are many Christians, so it wasn't a surprise to me that she was also a Christian. "He's going to live," she told me firmly. I wanted to believe her so badly, and something in her voice gave me strength to believe that he would. After seeing a specialist, who gave Errol some vitamin shots, my baby began to improve. Sadly, he would never be a normal, healthy boy. He struggled for the rest of his life with developmental challenges. To me, of course, he was always my beloved, beautiful, firstborn son.

Errol was born January 19, 1948, and my second son, Jeffrey, named for actor Jeffrey Hunter, was also born in 1948. You read that right: I bore two children in the year 1948! Jeffrey came just eleven months after Errol did, and was born on December 26th, my Christmas baby.

> While I was in labor, the dog snuck under my bed where he lay quietly. When Jeff was born, the dog came out from under the bed and barked in a friendly way.
>
> "Woof! Woof!" he barked in welcome, as if to say "Hello, hello! You're alive!"
>
> From then on we always called Jeff "Woof Woof."

With two babies so close together, I was a busy mom. Still, I had more support than most mothers do, at least for the time being. We had had servants before the concentration camp, and now in my married life I had them again. It seems like a dream now, but that's the way things were done in that time and place.

We had one servant for me, a dishwasher, a servant who did ironing and laundry, one for general housekeeping, one to do yard work, and a nanny for the children. And no, I can't remember what the servant did whose job it was to attend to me! It doesn't seem like there was much for her to do if all the dishes, laundry, housekeeping, yard work and childcare were already being done by other people!

Honestly, in those days, if you were middle class or above in Indonesia, you had this kind of support. Servants were incredibly inexpensive in that place and that time.

We had a female chef, too, and the kitchen was her domain. We all knew that we had better stay out of the kitchen if we knew what was good for us!

Cooking was one skill I possessed. I learned to cook when I was twelve years old. My mother taught me. She said, "I don't care if you are the queen or the president, you are going to learn to cook!"

In some ways it might appear as if we were living in the lap of luxury in a tropical paradise, but it was a very dangerous time for people of mixed Dutch ancestry to be living in our country of birth.

For years, a foundation of hatred and mistrust had been building between Indonesians and Indos. While I was in prison camp, there had been four registrations in which all Indos not enslaved already had to fill out their ethnic information.

The first three registrations gave the Japanese the intelligence they most wanted: people's ethnic makeup. The considerations that seemed most important were the color of the eyes and the color of the hair. Many women colored their hair black to indicate Indonesian roots. But the color of the eye could not be changed no matter how much some people wanted to change from black or brown to blue or green.

The fourth registration added a new question: Do you forsake the Dutch government and do you feel you are Asian?

Those who answered no would be captured, given ten guilders and allowed to take a suitcase to a small island where they had to try to survive. Many answered yes out of fear.

The Japanese motto during their occupation had been "Asia for Asians." Almost all Indonesians did *not* consider Indos to be Asian, and we increasingly felt as if we were strangers in our own home.

The Japanese propaganda during the war had stressed the poor relationship between Indonesians and Indos. They had been setting us up as bitter rivals, and it had worked all too well.

Rumors spread that the Indos were going to attack the Indonesians, and that the Indonesians had to be on guard. This was crazy! How could such a comparatively small group, now mostly made up of unarmed women, attack millions of Indonesians, many of whom had been issued weapons by the Japanese? Seeds had been intentionally planted for mass violence, which had already erupted all over the country.

The two ethnicities that ran through my blood were at war with each other.

By the time Japan surrendered on August 15, 1945, the relationship between Indos and Indonesians was boiling over. Indonesian nationalists intended to do anything they could to prevent the Dutch from reclaiming their colony. Two days later, on August 17, 1945, Sukarno had declared Indonesia's independence. The younger generation especially wanted a violent revolution, and bloodshed broke out everywhere as they shouted "Bersiap!" or "Be prepared" in Indonesian.

We Indos and ethnic groups such as the Dutch, Ambonese and Chinese were subject to intimidation, kidnapping, robbery, murder and organized massacres. Such attacks would continue throughout the course of the revolution, but had been most prevalent during the Bersiap period, from 1945-46.

The Indonesian struggle for independence would go on for four years, with untold lives lost on both sides. By the time the Netherlands officially transferred power to the new republic of Indonesia on December 27, 1949, the international community had swung over to the side of the extremists and had pressured the Dutch to give up their colony.

Those of us with Dutch blood were in more danger than ever. After the uprising and transfer of power in 1949, many Dutch and Indo Europeans, including us, decided to repatriate back to the Netherlands, our mother country. There we would finally be safe. There we would have a fresh start.

Before the concentration camp
1940

Top: Theodora, Mother Marie, Father Emile, Sister Theresia (Toet) and brother Ed.

Bottom left: Emile, father

Bottom right: Toet, Ed, Theodora

Toet (10), Ed (3), Theodora (11)
1937

Theodora & Lodewijk (John) Wedding Day 1946 (photo damaged in the flood)

Frits Philipus Oostvogels & Theodora Maria Oostvogels

Theodora, Mother Marie and Grandmother Theodora (Dora)

John in the military
1940

Theodora, Errol,
Shirley and Jeff
1950

Leaving Indonesia
1951

Uncle Rein,
Marie Oostvog
Shirley (baby)
Hank, Aunt T
Theodora, Err
and Jeff
1951

Mother Marie with Hank
The Netherlands
1956

Theodora
1956

Theodora and a friend
1956

Theodora, Mother Marie,
Sister Toet
1962

Theodora
1957

Theodora, John, Shirley, Roy, Dorris, Jeff and Glenn
1957

John (middle) and Theodora (bottom right)
with his Hawaiian band - 1958

Theodora with Neil's Thunderbird - 1963

Neil and Theodora on their wedding day, June 10, 1963 Salt Lake City, UT

Theodora & Neils's first time meeting sons- 1975
Clockwise: Neil, Glenn, Theodora, Roy & Jeff

Theodora and her
oldest son, Errol
1985

Errol, Jeff, Shirley, Theodora,
Roy, Glenn and Dorris - 1985

Glenn, Jeff, Roy, Dorris, Theodora,
Shirley and Irene - 2003

Mark and Dorris, Susy and Jeff, Shirley and Tony, Sheryl and Glenn, Irene and Roy, Theodora and Neil - 2003

Theodora and her oldest son, Errol 2004

50th Wedding Anniversary
June 10th, 2013

Grandson Theodore (Teddy) & Theodora
2015

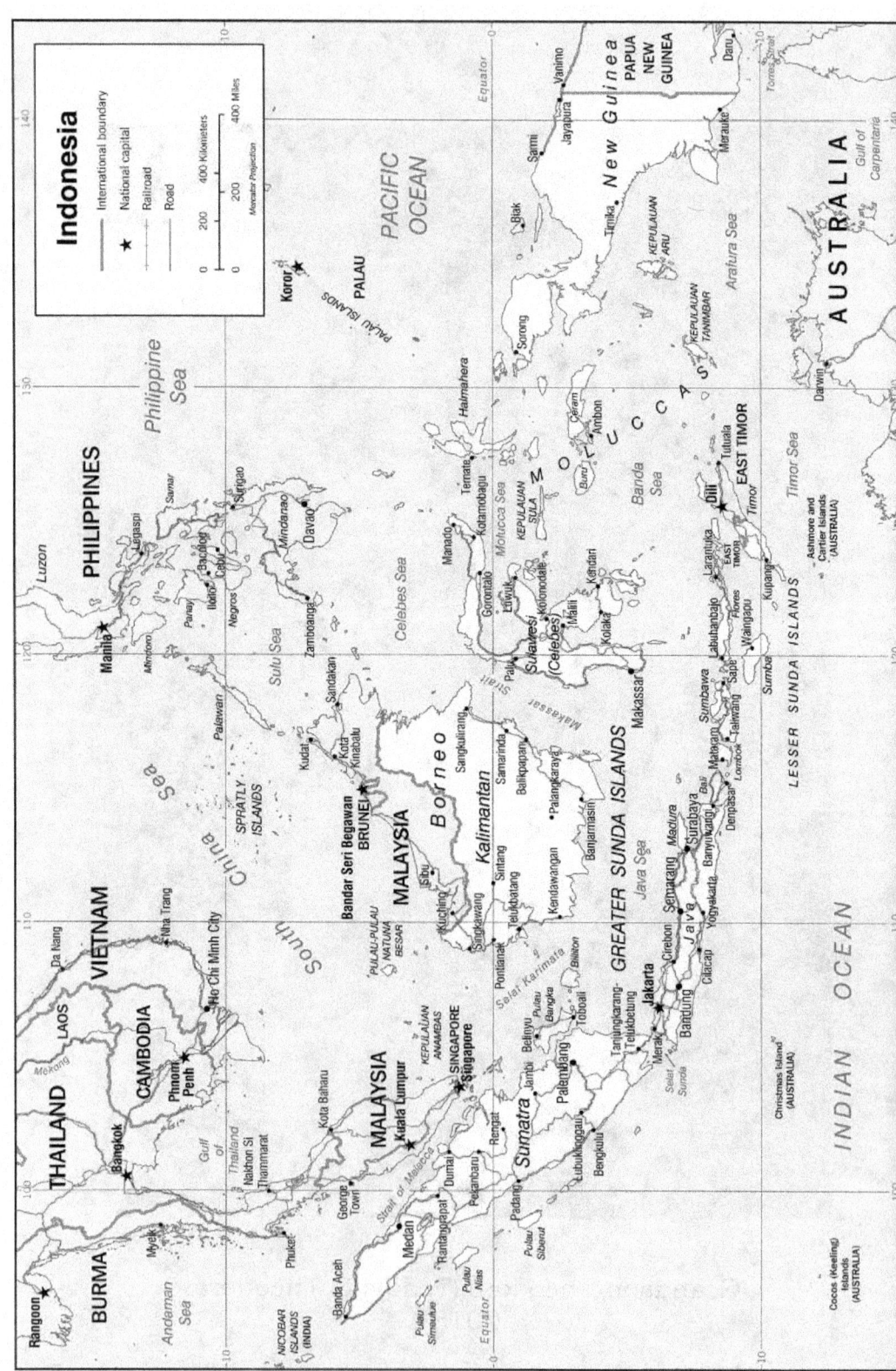

Chapter 9

I found out I was pregnant with Shirley just around the time John was transferred from Surabaya to Malang, my hometown. Shirley, named after Shirley Temple, was born in Malang on **April 26, 1950**.

By then there was absolutely no question that we had to find a way to leave. We had gotten several letters from the extremists.

"Get out now, or else," the letters said. "We have a tree picked out to hang all of you on it. Leave the country!"

There was the hammer and sickle symbol on each letter—the symbol of communism. I was petrified.

John didn't really want to leave, even though it was clear we had no choice. To add to our turmoil, the KNIL had folded when the Indonesians declared independence from the Dutch, effectively putting John out of a job. But nonetheless, we wanted to stay in Indonesia where it was warm and where John could hunt for wild boar.

He was in denial. The situation was live or die, leave or stay.

"You can stay, but I am leaving with the children with or without you," I finally said. I did not want to end up hanging on one of those trees.

I knew I had to do something. A friend of mine was headed for the Dutch consulate in Jakarta (formerly Batavia). I decided to join this friend on the twelve-hour journey from Malang to Jakarta by train. The servants watched my little ones while I was gone.

At the office of the Dutch consul, I presented the letters from the extremists as evidence that we were in grave danger.

"Mrs. Bodien, go home and wait for four days," they told me. "The military police will pick you up and take you to Surabaya and then Jakarta, and ultimately the Netherlands."

It all seemed very straightforward to me in that office, but I was later to learn that our motherland did not exactly welcome all of us with open arms. The country was already overpopulated and the job market overcrowded, and it was generally thought that the "Eastern Dutch," as we were being called, were very different (ie "foreign") and should therefore stay in Indonesia despite our Dutch blood.

By the time my first husband, our children and I would emigrate in 1950, there had already been one wave of emigration from Indonesia to the

Netherlands. The first wave, from 1925-1949, were mainly escaping from war, and most of these returned to Indonesia.

We were part of the second wave. This group, about 102,000 people, planned to stay in the Netherlands for the rest of our lives. This wave included many former military personnel and their families, which included us. There were in total six "waves," and 300,000 Indonesian Dutch who "repatriated" to the Netherlands. **Many people also went to Australia, Canada and the United States because they felt there was more opportunities there since there was high unemployment and a housing shortage after the war ended in Europe.**

Even if many in the government were resistant to welcoming hundreds of thousands of newcomers, quite a number of private aid organizations were formed to help the displaced Indos coming off boats and planes. The biggest need was for shelter. The number of exiles coming from Indonesia grew so large that the forty housing regions planned by the government proved to be inadequate. The government then started commissioning hotels and boarding houses.

However, as I stood in that office of the Dutch consul that day in Jakarta, I knew none of this. I only knew profound relief that this man in this uniform was telling me there was help coming.

Perhaps my family would be saved from the wrath of the nationalists.

We waited four days and, sure enough, the military police arrived to help us escape. We left with the clothes on our backs. We first fled from Malang to Surabaya.

John and I, along with our two boys and baby Shirley, got in a closed military Jeep. We were in a convoy traveling through a jungle area. Jeeps behind us were open and full of soldiers. The extremists were up in trees with guns. At one point, I heard gunfire and then screaming. A soldier in one of the Jeeps had been shot in the leg. "Don't stop!" my husband cried, and our Jeeps kept trundling through the jungle as we fled fresh violence.

We went to Surabaya and then Jakarta, where we stayed for a month in a Dutch camp.

And then it was time to leave our homeland for our motherland, probably forever. We boarded a ship bound for the Netherlands, filled with relief and some anxiety about the unknown. The ship was called the **Groote Beer.**

It was our exodus, however strange it felt to be on that ship and knowing that we didn't belong completely to either country. We were too Asian for the Netherlands, with our strange customs, foods, and tropical island ways. But we were no longer welcome in Indonesia, either, not by a long shot.

We stopped in Arabia, in Egypt's Port Said. Everyone got off except for me. I had developed terribly painful boils and had to stay on board with the baby. I believe the boils were caused by the drastic change in diet, from rice and vegetables to bread, potatoes, gravy, and fatty meat. That was the fare onboard.

I watched through a port hole on the ship as my friends disembarked, their feet on solid ground. I watched them with their shopping bags full and felt completely bereft.

After a month at sea we arrived in the port city of Rotterdam, the Netherlands. From the ship, I saw a man pushing a plow over some farmlands. He was the first white person I had ever seen doing manual labor.

I always said it was a hullaballoo getting ourselves to the Netherlands and, boy, was it ever. It was winter when we arrived in the longed-for homeland of my grandfathers and ancestors going back centuries. It was our safe harbor, but still cold and strange and unknown. We were foreigners there.

When we got off the ship, there was chaos everywhere. It was bitterly cold, and we were all very hungry. For some reason food was only being distributed to the officers and their families. Since my husband had recently left the KNIL, we got nothing. I told him, "Wait here with the children. I am going to find food for them." There was a Red Cross station right there at the port, and when I told them I had three little ones, they gave me mashed potatoes, meat, and mixed vegetables. Also, warm clothes and blankets.

The government housed us all in one room in Rotterdam. The next day we were sent by boat to Zeeland, in the far south, and we were again settled in one room of a hotel. Even though I felt an overwhelming sense of relief that we were finally safe from the extremists, living in one room with five people eventually started to make me feel stir crazy.

One day a social worker came and visited with us.

"How are you doing, Mrs. Bodien?" he asked me. "Not so good," I told him. "It's driving me nuts living in these cramped quarters! We need a house as soon as possible."

There I was being bold and gutsy again. I got it from my mother.

"You're in luck," he said. "We just finished a house (for displaced repatriates) in Kruiningen." And so our family of five soon moved into our first Dutch home. The government rented the house for us and gave us a modest stipend for food, clothing, and other living expenses. John was hired to do manual labor, digging potatoes, which was work to be sure but not what he was used to. He had been in a position of authority in the KNIL, so digging potatoes was a big step down. Yet in many ways we were far ahead. We were safe, and that counted for everything. Well, almost everything.

My mother and Hank—the man she had met on a ship to the Netherlands and with whom she would be in a warm, companionable relationship for the rest of their lives—had already been settled in The Hague for about a year. Hank was always kind to us—a father figure. I was glad my mother had found such a companion, though the two of them could never marry because marriage would have cut off her pension from my father. This was a fairly common business in those days, with widowed folks who wanted to be together yet couldn't afford to be married and lose their first spouse's pension.

My sister, **Toet, was established in Breda in the province of North Brabant. My brother Ed also had repatriated to The Netherlands and ended up living with my mother and Hank in The Hague. My mother, Hank, Toet, her husband and Ed came by train to visit us as often as they could.

Kruiningen was built on one of the islands that later formed Zuid-Beveland. The area was diked by monks of the abbeys of Ten Duinen and Ter Doest. (Later Kruiningen was to be hit hard during the flood of 1953.) There was a beautiful ancient church in the village, Johanneskerk, which was rebuilt in the 15th and 16th centuries after a fire in the 14th century.

The first time it snowed hard—as in, the snow was really coming down—I thought it was so beautiful. I went out in my bare feet and tried to catch the feathery clumps of snow as they fell from the sky. I tasted the snow, which was fresh and clean. My neighbor across the street started tapping on her window urgently. I looked up and she motioned for me to go inside. I think I was making her cold by standing there in my bare feet in the snow!

We settled into a new happiness and a new normal. Other Indos and people of mixed ancestry said they experienced racial bullying and slurs, but I never did. My neighbors were so kind to me. One neighbor taught me to make sauerkraut, and another how to do my laundry. We had always had servants until **the war broke out** and then again after the concentration camp, so I didn't know that I was supposed to separate out whites and colors. At first, my neighbors saw my sheets flapping on the clothesline in every color of the rainbow.

As you may know, the Dutch are known for their incredible cleanliness. Have you ever heard the saying "Dutch clean?" I had a lot to learn and often felt like I had two left hands when it came to keeping house.

But my neighbors were so nice to me, inviting me frequently for coffee and teaching me all the ways to be "Dutch clean." Once a week we would hang our rugs over the line and beat them hard to shake all the dirt off them. Think of the cleanest house and neatest yard you have ever seen. I guarantee the houses and yards in Kruiningen were cleaner and neater! We would sweep and mop and scrub *everything*. We even washed the sidewalk with soapy water!

Though we were newcomers on the island of Zuid-Beveland, we loved to entertain and frequently would open our home on a weekend night, inviting young people over to dance and listen to John's music. We would move the furniture to the corner and dance all night long.

Interestingly, our bathhouse was communal, in a separate building a few blocks away. We would walk down there about once a week to bathe at 25 cents a pop. In those days people in our village did not have separate bathtubs in their homes. Can you imagine a communal bathing situation in this day and age?

As much as I quickly grew to like and even love the Netherlands, I was still homesick for Indonesia. This lasted about a year in its most intense form, and to this day in a more manageable variety. I missed the more free, open, tropical island way of living, and I pined for the fresh fruits and vegetables there. I dreamed of the juicy papayas and mangoes especially.

My neighbor taught me how to plant a vegetable garden, which helped. We sprinkled seed for red cabbage, rhubarb, green beans, kale (we needed the kale for *Boerenkool*, after all) and carrots and enjoyed a harvest in its due time. I gained satisfaction out of growing food for my family, and grew to adore Dutch foods such as *Olliebollen*, a Dutch donut, or a deep-fried pastry filled with raisins and dusted with powdered sugar. But for a long while I craved the foods of my birth country, the country that had seemed to turn on me and so many of its other daughters and sons.

I longed for *Bami Goreng* with peanut sauce, egg rolls, fried rice, curried, spicy meats—the foods I grew up with that were no longer accessible to me in Europe. There was no doubt that I had gained a wonderful haven for me and my family, which now included Baby Roy, named after cowboy star Roy Rogers and born March 6, 1952—our Dutch boy. Yes, all the hullabaloo had been worth it. But I had lost a great deal as well. It would take me years to figure out how much.

Chapter 10

On the morning of February 1, 1953, our lives would be plunged into grave danger once again. Our haven would turn into a hellish nightmare.

We were fast asleep in our beds when we were awakened by loud pounding on our door. John hurried downstairs where he flung open the door to reveal one very panicked neighbor. He was terrified as he told John that the dam had broken and water was flooding quickly into our area. It would be at our door in half an hour or less.

John ran upstairs yelling. "Hurry up! There's a flood coming! We have to get out right now!"

My family and community was about to face the 1953 North Sea flood, the "Watersnoodramp" in Dutch, which literally translates to "water emergency disaster." There had been heavy storms the night before, but nothing so bad that it worried us. We had all gone to bed quite peacefully, blissfully unaware of what was headed our way.

Later we learned that there had been a deadly combination of a high spring tide and a severe European windstorm over the North Sea, which led to water levels of more than 18.4 feet above sea level in some locations. The flood and waves overwhelmed sea defenses and caused extensive flooding in our country, with 20 percent of its territory below sea level and 50 percent less than 3.3 feet above sea level. Many dykes proved unable to withstand the torrential waters and collapsed immediately.

Of all the nations affected by the flood, the Netherlands was worst affected, recording 1,836 deaths and widespread property damage. Most of the deaths and damage occurred in our province of Zeeland.

All told, 2,551 were killed—1,836 in the Netherlands, 307 in England, 28 in Belgium, 19 in Scotland, and 361 at sea. Nine percent of total Dutch farmland was flooded, 30,000 animals drowned, 47,300 buildings damaged of which 10,000 were destroyed. It was a disaster of epic proportions, and something none of us would ever be able to forget. Many people still commemorate the dead each February 1.

However, at that moment when John and I were scurrying around our house gathering our children as fast as we could, we knew none of the details. We only knew the flood was coming right for us.

It's funny the things that stick in your mind about a traumatic event that happened long ago. Oddly, I remember that I wanted to save my lovely chickens! But they were far less important than my four children! My first instinct was to get the little ones dressed and out of the house. But where I would take them I had no idea.

I just rushed around trying to get the children up and ready. I remember John saying that he wanted to run downstairs and save his tools, but there was no time for my chickens or his tools. We grabbed the kids and ran up to the top story of the house where we glued ourselves to the window. We were horrified by what we saw: a deluge of water, water everywhere. We wondered if Noah and his ark would glide by us at any minute.

Within seconds of seeing the flooding outside we heard all the windows on the first floor shattering as tons of water poured inside. It sounded for all the world as if the ocean had pushed its way into my house. From the window we could see pigs, cows, dogs and cats floating in a sea of bodies.

We heard one of our neighbors screaming for help but there was nothing we could do. We were trapped in our own home, not knowing if we would all drown within moments.

John and I grabbed a bunch of blankets and carried the kids up to the attic, which was the highest point of our house. There was a window in the attic and we could see the water rising by inches below us. We had no idea whether the water would stop rising before it overtook us. Would we all die in a watery grave?

Errol and Jeff were crying; they were frightened and could probably pick up on our fear, too.

Honestly, I was more scared in those moments in a Dutch attic than I was when I was forced to go to a concentration camp. For one thing, I was very young at the time and it didn't seem possible that the prison camps could be that bad. (I didn't know then I would lose my father and almost starve.)

Now I was a mother of four and my children were vulnerable. At camp we had each other and lots of other fellow prisoners, but in that cold attic it was just my family and I, alone to face the potentially deadly torrent. I looked at my children, who were so small and defenseless. There was no way for me to save my little ones if it came to that. They could be swept away by these horrific waters and there would be nothing I could do to prevent it.

My life prayer arose in me. "God help me, help us!" A deep certainty settled over my spirit in that moment. Though I was still scared, I suddenly knew that we would make it no matter what. After surviving the Japanese concentration camp and fleeing the Indonesian nationalists, I felt sure my growing family would survive this catastrophe, too.

In the Netherlands the houses were set very close together, so close that our neighbor was able to slide some bread to us over a wood plank he stretched between his window and ours. He knew we had little ones who were hungry. Of course, hunger was the least of our problems.

After a few hours in the attic, John, watching the situation outside through the attic window, noticed that the water seemed to be receding a bit. "Must be the tide," we decided with great relief. He told me to stay put with the children while he went down to see what state our house was in below.

When he gave me the all clear, I carefully climbed down the attic stairs holding baby Roy. I helped the other children climb down too, and told them to be careful. I made sure to bring the blankets.

What we saw was beyond my wildest imagination. Even on our second floor, the water was up to the middle of the windows. All our belongings—furniture, clothing, books, photos—were drifting on top of the water.

The water began to recede with the tide, and was lowest in the bathroom and the hall, where John spotted a boat speeding toward us through the window. The people on the boat were motioning for us. "Come, come! We are here to rescue you!"

Sloshing through the water one by one, with me carrying the baby, our family got to the window, which was hopefully going to be our portal to safety.

John's mother was six feet tall—a big lady (she too had come from Indonesia in 1952 and moved in with my family). She was trembling in fear at the thought of jumping out the window into the boat. "Please! Please, let me just stay here and die!" she was wailing.

Of course we were never going to let that happen.

With our hearts in our throats, we bundled baby Roy up and dropped him out the window into the outstretched arms of the rescuers. Then, one by one, Shirley, Jeff, and Errol were lowered and then dropped into the rescue boat. Can you imagine as a mother literally dropping your children out a window? It was extremely frightening but I knew this was our only chance to be rescued.

My mother-in-law was still highly agitated about jumping. Finally John told her that if she didn't jump he would conk her on the head. "Then you'll be unconscious and have no choice!" he yelled at her. Sounds harsh, but he was desperate.

I'll never forget this for as long as I live: My mother-in-law wanted to jump headfirst into the boat! It still makes me giggle to think about that strapping lady preparing to dive in, plunging like she was an Olympic swimmer! She sat on the windowsill trying to summon the courage to jump. We were running out of time. I gave her a little push on her back and took the decision right out of her hands! Well, she was safe and that was the main thing. (And in case you were wondering, I loved my kind mother-in-law! You know what they say about desperate times...)

I jumped next, and finally John. Our entire family had literally leapt out the window, leaving our home for good. There was no turning back. There was no saving our home. We didn't know it then but we would end up living in another town in the aftermath of the flood. But in that moment, all we cared about was getting our children to dry land.

As we sped off in the boat, I could hardly believe my eyes. Yesterday we had walked around the neighborhood going about our usual business, but just one day later everything had changed. It was as if we had been transported in our sleep to a strange, nightmarish water-world. Our community was halfway under water, and there were motorboats everywhere trying to rescue as many people as they could.

Most of our neighbors were rescued but we did lose two friends, a father and son. Their family worked for a bus company and they were trying to move the buses and salvage them ahead of the flood. But Jan and his son were carried away in the flood and drowned like so many others. It was a terrible tragedy for Jan's wife, who had lost both husband and son. Sad to say so many stories ended like theirs. Our village of Kruiningen alone lost sixty-two people that terrible day.

We were chugging along in the rescue boat for only about fifteen minutes when we were taken to the village church, *Johanneskerk*, which sat on the highest point in the area. I distinctly remember walking by that church when we first arrived in the village. It was dark outside, and I peeked in the windows to see the people inside dressed in all black. It had given me an eerie feeling and I had wondered what kind of church it was.

It was freezing in the boat, so I was thankful I had grabbed those blankets.

By the time we got to the church, aid efforts had been somewhat organized. There was warm clothing and shoes for us and the children. Remember, we had been woken by the flood in the night and were barefoot. People packed in the church but there was food for all of us.

We were told we would be taken to Goes (pronounced "Hoos") and resettled there for the time being. Within a few hours the water ebbed enough that we could travel by large truck to Goes. The truck was open air and I wrapped the children in the blankets again as we lumbered down watery roads to our next destination. We were all bleary eyed and stunned by the last twenty-four hours, marveling at our close call with death and disoriented by the succession of drastic changes. Therefore it was somewhat calming to arrive in Goes, where a friend offered to take our family in. For the next month or two we stayed in one room of their house. It was cramped but, again, we were safe and that was all that mattered.

Meanwhile my mother and sister, who lived in areas of the country not affected by the flood, were scared by what they were hearing about the rising death toll in our region. They called the Red Cross, which was eventually able to tell them that me and my family were all in one piece.

From Goes and our friend's home, Toet and her husband took us into their home in Breda for six months. It was a happy time for the most part. Toet's kids were around the same age as my kids so the cousins all played together and kept each other occupied. But at the same time, this period was filled with the anxiety of the unknown.

There were so many questions. For one, where would we be living? The government of the Netherlands faced another housing crises as tens of thousands of people were displaced by the flood. John finally went to the government and pushed the fact that we needed a home of our own. After six months we moved back to Goes, not back to our village of Kruiningen. It took a whole year for the clean-up crews to get rid of all the water and rebuild our wonderful little town, yet we had to move forward with the business of living.

Goes was a bigger municipality, also in Zeeland, and now inhabited by about 27,000 people. Our new town boasted a graceful, circular harbor lined with very old, picturesque buildings with the classic stepped gables of 17th century Dutch architecture. For several years we found a refuge in Goes and added two more children to our growing family.

Little did I know that my family was not really safe at all. In the not-too-distant future, our happiness would be threatened again not by war, violent uprisings, or natural disaster, but by the betrayal of someone closest to me.

Chapter 11

Our family grew up a little bit in the years after we settled in Goes. Glenn, named after musician, arranger and composer Glenn Miller, was born August 13, 1954, and Dorris, named for actress Doris Day, was born March 8, 1956. They were both adorable babies, and I loved the joy and sweetness they brought to our family. As it turned out, I needed all the sweetness I could get.

I found out John was cheating on me. This revelation, after everything else that had happened to me, was like a grenade tossed in the middle of my home. The ripple effects were to extend deep and wide through the rest of my life, and the lives of my children.

When we moved to Goes, John had taken a job as a bookkeeper for a businessman. The businessman had a daughter named Toes (pronounced like "Toast"). Toes was at least twenty years younger than John, so I never suspected anything was going on between them. Why would I?

John eventually got a job in Rotterdam, the port city into which we had immigrated to the Netherlands more than six years previously. He would go and work there on weekdays and come home for weekends. What I didn't know was that

Toes had followed him there and the two of them were sharing his small apartment.

During this time, Errol's developmental challenges had become harder and harder to handle. He was eight years old, and would play roughly with the other boys in the neighborhood. I loved him dearly but had no idea how to help or manage him sometimes.

Everything came to a head one day when Errol snuck a kitchen knife out of our drawer at home and was flashing it around at other boys in the schoolyard. In those days social workers who would ride bicycles around areas where children were playing, observing them and watching for signs of trouble. There was a young woman social worker who happened to be riding her bike by the schoolyard, and she witnessed Errol threatening the other boys with a knife. She found out where he lived and came over to talk to me that day.

"Your son should be placed in a home where they can help him and care for his special needs," she told me kindly. "He is becoming dangerous to himself and others."

She told me about a good home run by the Catholics where Errol could live in safety and be well cared for. But I wasn't ready for that yet.

I was devastated, full of worry about my son. John was little help to me. He was gone most of the time and when he was home he was often physically and emotionally abusive.

I frantically searched for a solution. Maybe if we all immigrated to the United States, we could be together as a family and my son could also get the help he needed. The Dutch government was offering money to those who would consider immigrating. At the time the country was badly overcrowded and there were not enough jobs or houses to go around. It was post-war and post-flood, and things were a mess. Could we find new hope as a family in a new country?

I talked to John about immigrating, and he agreed. And then I found out about **Toes, through a friend of John's.**

John, evidently somewhat burdened with guilt, talked his best friend Jeff into trying to seduce me. He must have figured that if I succumbed, then we would be on an even playing field and he wouldn't have to feel so guilty.

Jeff lived in Rotterdam near where John lived during the week. John brought him home for the weekend to Goes, hoping his plan would work.

One evening John was playing music for a bunch of people and Jeff asked me to dance. We danced literally a few feet away from where John was singing. I could tell Jeff was attracted to me, which was flattering but also made me a little bit uncomfortable. He asked to talk to me privately so we went somewhere to talk. Jeff told me he was falling in love with me and wanted me. "Absolutely not," I protested. "I am a married woman!"

"Oh, are you *really*?" Jeff replied. "You *think* you are a married woman, but let me tell you about your husband..."

He told me about John and Toes and their affair. At first I didn't believe him. I didn't want to believe him, but something deep inside me confirmed that this was true.

"If you don't believe me, come to Rotterdam and see for yourself," Jeff said. I arranged for childcare for my six children and traveled to Rotterdam with my heart in my throat.

On my way to John's apartment, I spotted him and Toes walking arm and arm together, smiling like lovers in their own little world. My world as I knew it cracked wide open. In a state of shock, I followed them to his apartment, waited for them to get nicely inside, and then threw open the door. He was stunned, of course, to see his wife and the mother of his children burst through the door of his love nest. I was ablaze with anger and hurt.

"How could you do this to me?" I demanded. "We have children!" When Toes scuttled out of there in a hurry, John and I were left alone to confront the ruins of our marriage.

"I want a divorce," he told me finally. "I have fallen in love with Toes and out of love with you."

"Why, *why* didn't you tell me this before I had all of these children with you?" I was horrified at his betrayal as the reality began to dawn on me: My marriage was ending and I would be alone with six children under the age of eight.

He really didn't have much to say for himself. "I don't know..." was his feeble response. John wanted to have his cake and eat it too. Later I would realize this scenario had played out in a similar way when we first met, me as a young girl and he as the older, married man. I wondered, did Toes buy his lies as easily as I did?

That night I stayed with Jeff in his apartment because it was too late to return to Goes. Nothing happened except my tears and Jeff's comfort, although later I turned to him out of desperation and, yes, revenge.

I returned to Goes and my children with a heavy heart. As I processed the devastation I was feeling, the reality remained that Errol needed special care. He had also stolen apples from a farmer's orchard and the farmer caught him and spanked him. My son was out of control.

I prayed that God would help me once again. I began to feel that immigration to the United States was the right course of action. There would be so many more opportunities for my children there, and we all needed a fresh start. Not that I thought my marriage would be saved by a boat ride across the ocean. I knew in my heart it was over. But I could not immigrate as a single mother, and so John agreed to join us. His plan was to immigrate with me and the kids and then send for Toes.

We slept together infrequently after that, but soon I learned I was pregnant with my seventh child. With God's help, this child would be born in the United States—an American.

There was one big obstacle between us and the Promised Land—would Errol be allowed to come with us?

As part of the immigration process, we all had to undergo physical exams and be evaluated as far as our mental fitness. Even the children were examined for any physical or mental problems, and Errol could not pass that test. We were notified that all of us were cleared for immigration, except for Errol. They had sent us a kind letter to that effect, but their kindness could not protect me from the most agonizing decision of my life.

I was shattered. My darling firstborn son! How could I possibly leave him in the Netherlands while we moved an ocean away?

It was an impossible decision for any mother to make. I prayed for wisdom, and two thoughts kept coming to me. First, my other five (really six) children would be privy to a world of opportunity in the United States, the chance to dream their dreams and see them fulfilled. There was nothing for them in the Netherlands, at least not at that time. Second, I had visited the Catholic home for developmentally challenged children and I could see with my eyes and my heart that Errol would be lovingly cared for there. And, I figured, we could visit him from time to time. I don't think I realized how truly far away we would be.

I made the excruciating decision to proceed with immigration and leave Errol in the care of the Catholic home. Even though I knew he would get the help he needed there—help I could not give him—the pain of leaving him behind was beyond anything I could imagine. The day we drove to the home to take Errol there was probably the worst day of my life, and I have had many terrible days. Try as I might, I could not make him understand what was happening. All he knew was that he was being left in a strange place with strange people, and his Mommy and Daddy and sisters and brothers were all driving away without him.

In my mind, I can still hear his screams as he clung to me, begging me not to leave him. "Don't leave me, Mama! Don't leave me!!" Young mothers say it is wrenching to leave their children in daycare or church nursery, especially when they are crying for mama. This experience was that scenario times a hundred. I felt physically ripped in two when I finally managed to disentangle myself from Errol's frantic limbs and flee to the car. It was sixty years ago, and that goodbye still haunts me. It always will.

Chapter 12

I was pregnant with my seventh child while I grieved leaving behind my first as we crossed the Atlantic Ocean to the United States **on board the Zuiderkruis.** John and I were barely speaking, tolerating each other as co-parents and sort of partners in the immigration process. On February 27, 1957, we reached New York City, then docked in Hoboken, New Jersey where we were processed as emigres to a new land. We took the city bus to a restaurant and then to the train station.

From New York we traveled via train to Grand Rapids, Michigan, a Midwest city with a large Dutch immigrant population. Our family had been sponsored by Third Reformed Church, which provided us with an apartment, basic household amenities such as towels and dishes, and used toys for the children to play with. The church also arranged for John to work in a furniture factory. We thought the church was very kind to do all of this for us, but we were in a lot of turmoil and the dark, gloomy apartment on Sherman Street did not help. My life was in pieces; a new continent and a bewildering, new language only added to the unrest.

Within a few weeks, the church moved us to a brighter apartment directly across the street from the old one. Physically things were brighter, but emotionally my outlook was darker than ever. I was terribly sad about Errol and pregnant with my seventh child, whose future was so unclear. My marriage was now a broken, unfixable thing.

The older children did not adjust well to their new country at first. Roy and Jeff were called names because they wore knickers like the little Dutch boys they were. But the boys at school called them "Mexican" because of their dark Indo skin and hair. Dutch Mexicans? I guess it made as much sense as Dutch Indonesians. This persecution was a little surprising because Henry School was quite integrated for that time period, being an inner-city school mixed with whites and African Americans.

Soon after we immigrated, a woman named Marie **(her first name has been changed here to protect our family from possible reprisals from her children),** from the Dutch Immigrant Society came over to help me get settled. She had come herself from the Netherlands a few years before and was bilingual at that point, which was extremely helpful. I could barely speak a word of English and was floundering in my new surroundings.

Irene was born on August 1, 1957, our only American child by birth. I always adored being pregnant, but this was the end of that road for me! I was thirty-one years old and had delivered seven babies in eight and a half years.

We were very poor, so it was a struggle to buy enough cow's milk for the baby to drink. There was no such thing as formula in those days. Irene ended up being a good, strong girl, but I worried that she was not getting adequate nutrition. I supplemented her diet with rice milk and homemade baby food.

Marie whose husband was Indo, helped me with that and so many other things including housework and caring for my six children. She had two children of her own, but I dearly needed the help and appreciated having a new friend in a strange land, especially one who was fluent in Dutch.

Since my marriage was over before we set foot in the United States, it wasn't a big shock when I learned that Marie was having an affair with John. Ever the musician, he had quickly formed a band in Grand Rapids and befriended Marie's husband, going so far as to teach him how to play bongos and put him in the band. (Don't feel too sorry for Marie's husband. He was cheating on her, too!)

When we departed for the U.S., John had left a heartbroken **Toes behind. She had become ill and could not join him in America after all. She was still writing him love letters by the time he took up with Marie, and the two of them would read Toes's letters in bed. Marie told me this, laughing, and I was so far past caring about John's love life that I laughed along with her! I know it sounds crazy but that's the way things were then—crazy!

But even as Marie and I were laughing together as we chatted or shopped or cleaned the apartment, something was rotten in Denmark. I still find it hard to reconcile my fun, helpful friend with what happened next.

As her relationship with John intensified, our divorce was in the process of becoming a reality. Even though I felt vulnerable in a new country in which everyone spoke this foreign language, I wanted to go through with the divorce. Any love John and I had shared was by then extinguished by the chronic abuse and infidelity. Although I think that if he had not been abusing me I would have stayed for the children's sake.

I did not speak English, nor did John, but Marie did and she used this to her great advantage. She knew I had no idea about my rights in terms of child support or custody. She saw an opportunity to swoop in and take what was rightfully mine. She spotted the chance to send another wrecking ball through my life.

By this time she and her husband were divorced, and she was free to become John's fourth wife. She whispered in his ear how he could get away from me for good and not have to pay me a dime of child support. Marie connived to find a way to ensure John would also have full custody and I would have nothing.

The two of them hired a lawyer and finagled to have me labeled an "unfit" mother. (I puzzled over that description for years, believing it was a statement about my physical health! I only realized what that word really meant a few years ago when Shirley finally explained it to me.)

No lawyer or social worker came to assess whether I was "fit" or not. The law just took Marie and John at their word. Without knowing what I was doing, I signed away rights to my children. All I knew was that I could not speak English, I had no money, no skills, and there was no way I could take care of them. I was unaware that I could have received child support and kept at least partial custody, and no one thought to tell me otherwise.

By the time all was said and done and I drove away from my children for what would be many years, it was 1959. Jeff was eleven, Shirley was nine, Roy was seven, Glenn was five, Dorris was three and Irene was just a baby. And my precious Errol was twelve, living an ocean away from me.

I was in terrible, desperate pain but didn't think I had any options. I could see no way out of the mess my life had become. Sometimes at night, when I would lie awake pining for them, I would hear them crying for me. Or maybe what I heard was me, crying for them.

Chapter 13

There were angels along the way, even in my bleakest days. Broke and desperate, I spotted a want ad for a masseuse in the newspaper (I had taken some training in the Netherlands) and decided to show up at the office and ask for a job. Things were so bad that I got into the cab knowing I had no money to pay for the ride. When we arrived at the address in the want ad, I confessed to the cab driver that I had no way to pay him. To my shock and relief, he looked at me and smiled. "This is a free ride," he said. "Call me when you are done and I will pick you up, too."

The interview, if you can call it that, was not the total bust it might have been considering I had misinterpreted the ad, which was for a chiropractic office and not a masseuse! It helps to know the language of a want ad when you answer it! But the chiropractor was also kind and he suggested I contact his cousin, Hazel, who might have some work for me.

Hazel was my angel. A middle-aged, wealthy woman with a heart of gold, Hazel hired me as her maid, even giving me a black maid's uniform in which to dust and sweep. It was ironic that I, the woman who once had more servants than she knew what to do with, was now grateful to be someone else's servant.

Hazel was also a Christian and a member at LaGrave Avenue Christian Reformed Church. She became like a mother to me, watching out for me as my own mother in the Netherlands could not. She also owned a beauty salon and a beauty school, which I gravitated to like a moth to a flame. When Hazel noticed the way my eyes would sparkle and my energy would lift around all things beautiful, she invited me to become a student there for free. Truly, Hazel brought me up in the beauty business and taught me everything I know.

Though I walked every step with a hole in my heart, beauty school was a surprising comfort and joy. I enjoyed everything about it—from learning how to cut, color and perm hair to hanging out with my lively young fellow students. I still did not know English but, apparently, I possessed an instinct for making others look their most beautiful.

On breaks from school, I would walk over to the coffee shop next door. This is where I met a man named "Root," who could spot easy prey when he saw it. Despite the small buds of hope that were opening at beauty school, my life was mostly in ashes. I was at my most vulnerable, looking for someone to rescue me, to throw me a rope when I was drowning.

Unfortunately, what this man threw me was less a rope and more a chain. I was so beaten down I couldn't see it. I couldn't see him for what he was, which was a cruel con artist.

The less said about Root the better, but suffice to say he talked me into marrying him within a month or two of our first meeting. After three months he began abusing me, and after six months of marriage he told me he was bisexual and wanted an "open marriage." I already hated him, so I didn't much care if he was interested in being with me or not.

For some reason, he became most violent when we were driving somewhere. He would strike me in the face at stoplights or threaten to throw me out of the car. I remember I had to wear sunglasses to my beauty school exam because I was afraid my friends would see my bruises. I was so miserable I considered throwing myself out of the car and ending it all. But my childhood faith stood me in good stead. When I prayed "Jesus, help me," I knew in the pit of my soul that God wanted me to live.

Root and I were renting a room from a nice old grandfather who had a house on Plainfield Avenue in Grand Rapids. There were others who boarded at this house, including a young Dutch man who would bring his friends over to socialize.

One day he brought a friend named Neil Kleisma to the house, and we hit it off right away. Neil was an airplane technician, a recent immigrant from the Netherlands, and both of us were homesick (yes, now I was also homesick for the Netherlands!). We were eager to talk about everything "back home." He had come to the U.S. the year before me so things were confusing and strange to him, too.

We bonded in the way that expats from the same country always do, and soon I found myself telling him about my marriage troubles with Root. "I want to get away from him," I told Neil. "He is so abusive."

Neil himself had witnessed Root hitting me at the house on Plainfield, so he readily believed me and wanted to help. At that time, my mother back in the Netherlands had to have an operation and I dearly wanted to fly back and be with her. Neil, who had worked for KLM airlines for many years and was currently working for Lear, loaned me the money.

If I am honest, I started to develop feelings for Neil the moment I met him. I was married to a monster and here was Neil, a Dutchman who was kind to me and seemed to offer an escape route. Neil returned my feelings and told me he wanted to marry me. We talked about how I could get away from Root, physically and legally, and hatched a plan.

I managed to play on Root's fragile ego, convincing him that he would be much happier as a single person without a wife to complicate his life. We began divorce proceedings, which went quite quickly. In the meantime, Neil and I were planning a getaway. I honestly worried that, even after we were divorced, Root might find me and hurt me—or worse—if I stayed in the city of Grand Rapids.

Neil got a job at a military air base in Utah, and the minute the divorce was final the two of us jumped in his gleaming green, late 1950s Ford Thunderbird and drove west. We were both so proud of that car!

Yes, I was leaving my children behind. But I was not allowed to see them. Being so close and yet so far from them was killing me. I carried them with me in my heart. How could I not?

I was also leaving behind tremendous pain and danger in our rear-view mirror. I had written Root a "Dear John" letter, stating clearly that I never loved him. "Don't find me," the letter warned.

For the first time in years, I felt free.

In Salt Lake City, I met up with distant relatives there and stayed with them briefly. Neil and I were married on June 10, 1963, by a Mormon priest. We could hear the Mormon Tabernacle Choir singing beautifully. I was thirty-six years old, and had already lived through several lifetimes on three separate continents. I was ready for a calm and steady life with a husband who would never hit me.

We settled in Ogden, Utah, by the base where Neil worked. One day we were enjoying a pretty day at a park when a man approached Neil.

"Can I give you a compliment?" he asked.

Both of us assumed immediately that he would pay Neil a compliment about the Thunderbird, which was parked nearby in the sunlight, shiny and impressive. We waited for the praise that was sure to come next.

"Sir, you have a beautiful wife!"

I still laugh when I think about the look on Neil's face!

We settled into married life together and were happy for the most part. Neil was a complex man and saw in me a "simple" woman who would not complicate his life, especially since my seven children were not able to live with me. He never foresaw that my children would reenter my life someday, and that's the way he preferred things to be.

"Try and forget about them," he would insist, as if I ever could. When he was working at night I would think about my children and sob, but I never did this in front of him.

Because of God, I forgave everyone who hurt me, including Neil. I forgave the Japanese, the Indonesian extremists, and John and Marie for taking my children away from me. I forgave myself for all the mistakes I had made. Despite everything that would go wrong with Neil much later on, I will always be grateful to him for caring for me. This enabled me to move forward in a way nothing else could.

We stayed in Utah for two years until then-Secretary of Defense Robert McNamara began to call for mass layoffs and Neil lost his job at the base.

He had no trouble landing another, especially with his KLM credentials, and was soon hired at United Airlines in the San Francisco Bay area. Although I was crazy about the Bay area, and California overall, I was a little bit bored doing nothing all day while I waited for Neil to get home from work. I decided it was time to retake my beautician's exam, which I had failed by 1.5 points the first time I had taken it in this new state. Boy, was I ever upset when I flunked that test! The second time I passed with a score of 80 percent, which I thought was pretty good considering I still didn't know much English! The beauty business called to me even in California, and I was eager to answer it.

I loved everything about working as a hairdresser. I enjoyed cutting people's hair and talking to them while they sat in my chair. I had taken additional massage classes, too, and was qualified to give massages. I would haul my massage table to rich women's mansions in the area and be paid a nice sum for working on their stiff muscles.

I used to go to the gilded Hearst Mansion and massage Patty Hearst's German caregiver! Patty Hearst, of course, is the heiress to the Hearst publishing fortune who was kidnapped in the 1970's by a left-wing terrorist group known as the Symbionese Liberation Army. Famously, she was later indoctrinated by them, joined their criminal activities and, in the notorious trial of the decade, tried and convicted as a bank robber.

There was no way of knowing that the little girl running around the house, playing dress-up with cut-up luxury garments from her mother's closet, would end up being one of the most infamous figures of her day! I would often be sent home by cab, with the German caregiver picking up the tab.

Life was good in sunny California. We also made some cherished new friends in the Bay area including an Indo couple called Gus and *Zus* (which means "sis" in English). Gus is widowed like me and we still talk on the phone at least once a week.

Neil and I were in California for about ten years when I received a piece of mail that would change everything, for it would eventually bring me back to the children I had loved and lost.

Chapter 14

Though I had left Grand Rapids about sixteen years beforehand, obviously I had never stopped thinking about the six people I loved there. I had kept in touch with Hazel and her daughter, Lucy, in the California years. One day I received a letter from Lucy, and folded inside was an obituary cut from the pages of *The Grand Rapids Press.*

My first husband, John, had died. It was 1975. My spine tingled when I read the names of my three daughters: Shirley, Dorris and Irene, and the name of a grandchild I didn't even know I had: Tammy.

It seemed odd to me that the boys' names were not included in the obituary, but later I discovered that the three boys—Jeff, Roy and Glenn—had been cut off from their father by Marie, their stepmother and my former friend. Marie had kept their names out of the obituary.

They were all grown now; even Irene was eighteen. Maybe now that John was out of the picture I could have a relationship with them. My heart pounded in my chest at the thought.

That night, I summoned the old gutsy Theodora and called Michigan with my heart in my throat. Lucy had sent me Jeff's phone number, so I called him first. His wife answered.

"Mom!" she immediately said, "where have you been?" It was so nice to meet my daughter-in-law over the phone.

The next day Jeff called me back. Hearing my son's voice after sixteen years was one of the most incredible experiences of my life. He was very warm to me, welcoming and loving. So were Roy and Glenn when they called me soon after. When I told Roy I was planning to come visit them, I said he wouldn't be able to recognize me.

"I would know you anywhere, mom," he said. My heart melted. Was this really happening? Was I about to gain back all the years that the locusts had stolen?

My perception at first was that my sons were more open to a relationship with me than my daughters, but in truth all my children struggled in their own ways to process my reentry into their lives. It would take years of healing for my relationships with my children to be restored.

When I flew into Detroit soon after that phone call, accompanied by Neil, I was greeted with open arms by my three sons. We bundled into someone's car and drove the two-plus hours back to Grand Rapids, a city I had once fled.

Unbeknownst to me, the boys were bugging Shirley to meet me. She remembered far more of me than her sisters, who were very young when I was forced to give them up. But she too had been raised mostly by Marie, who had poisoned them all against me.

Yet the boys were on the outs with Marie, who had treated them poorly and had not allowed them to visit their father on his deathbed. And Shirley's relationship with Marie was not close. Shirley was torn between two mothers—all the girls were—but she reluctantly agreed to come over to Jeff's house and bring her two sisters and her daughter along. Tammy kissed me on the cheek at that first meeting, and has owned a piece of my heart ever since.

We've all had our ups and downs in the forty-two years since that first reunion. I was overjoyed to be in their lives again but it would take lots of healing and grace for us to be close again. Only God could work that kind of redeeming miracle in our hearts.

Sad to say, Neil only hurt the process of rebuilding these relationships. He always saw the children as competition for my love, time and energy. If it had been up to him, I never would have seen them again. A staunch atheist, he railed against the strong Christian faith of especially Shirley and Tony, her husband. The man who had once encouraged me to forgive everyone was unwilling to open his heart to my children and grandchildren. This was his great loss, and he never realized it to the end of his life.

Still, in 2002 he agreed to move back to Grand Rapids and start a new life in retirement there. He grew more fractious by the year and was never friendly to my children. He didn't like it if I spent too much time with them, and I was definitely not allowed to go to church with them as they had invited me to do.

In fact, I couldn't even pray aloud in Neil's presence, a problem which only intensified as he got older and more stuck in his ways. Sometimes I would lie in bed and pray silently, begging God to help me stay strong as my husband of fifty-two years deteriorated and became harder to be around.

In 2004 my son Errol died, which I found nearly unbearable. I think of him every day and am so grateful I could fly to the Netherlands and visit him often, especially after Neil got the job with United Airlines. For years I would make the annual trip to my second homeland to visit my son. Wonderfully, his brothers and sisters also got to be reunited with him in the years between 1975 and his death.

On May 21, 2015, Neil died, leaving me a widow at the age of eighty-nine. I had loved him in life and grieved him in death, despite how difficult he had become. We had many good years together. Sometimes I find myself lonesome for him and other times I am relieved that he is gone.

As soon as he died, I started praying aloud again and also attending church with my daughters Shirley and Dorris and their husbands. To worship together with other believers from all over the world at Madison Square Christian Reformed Church is a great blessing to me in my final years of life.

At times I am able to go back in my memory and relive some of the things that happened to me. I remember how it felt to lose everything, first as a teenager, then as a young wife and mother, then a few years later in the flood, and finally the great loss of my children when I was in my early thirties.

But I'm still here, at age ninety-one, held up by God's right hand and holding on to His promises.

Yes, I lost everything, but today I stand before you having gained so much. My faith in my father's loving God has been boosted over and over, and I believe in Him more than ever. I also believe in the power of forgiveness. There's nothing like it to move mountains in your life that seem immoveable.

Dear reader, I thank you for listening to my account of one woman's near century of survival on three continents. I leave you with two pieces of advice that have made all the difference in my life and will make all the difference in yours:

Always pray, even if all you can say is "God help me!" He will. He always will.

And finally, forgive! Forgive everyone who has ever hurt you. Start by forgiving yourself. God protects. God loves. And God heals every wound. He has so many gifts to give.

Just ask the girl whose name means "gift of God."

Just ask me, Theodora.

Et}

Recipe for *Soto Ajam* (Dutch Indonesian Soup)

1 whole chicken

4 onions, sliced

2 cloves of garlic, minced

3 candlenuts (available in Asian markets, or substitute macadamia nuts)

2 tsp coriander

2 tsp turmeric

2 tsp lemongrass, peeled, sliced and pureed in a food processor

2 ounces celery, chopped

Half a white cabbage, sliced finely

6-ounce package bean sprouts

3 eggs, hardboiled and sliced

4 small potatoes, sliced

1 small can of French fried onions

Cooked white rice

Directions:

Boil the chicken

Saute herbs and garlic in oil

Throw the herbs in with the chicken

Remove and shred chicken, reserving broth

Serve steaming broth with white rice in bowls

Add chicken, fresh vegetables, and eggs to each bowl

Add Indonesian ketchup (Ketjap), Sambal, and Kroepoek shrimp crackers to taste.

www.ingramcontent.com/pod-product-compliance
Lightning Source LLC
Chambersburg PA
CBHW052148110526
44591CB00012B/1902